G. W. Leibniz *and* Samuel Clarke

Correspondence

G. W. Leibniz *and* Samuel Clarke

Correspondence

Edited, with Introduction, by

Roger Ariew

Hackett Publishing Company, Inc.
Indianapolis/Cambridge

For DBA, DAA, and SAA

Copyright © 2000 by Hackett Publishing Company, Inc.

All rights reserved

Printed in the United States of America

10 09 08 07   2 3 4 5 6 7 8

For further information, please address:
  Hackett Publishing Company, Inc.
  P. O. Box 44937
  Indianapolis, IN 46244–0937

www.hackettpublishing.com

Cover design by Listenberger Design & Associates

Library of Congress Cataloging-in-Publication Data

Leibniz, Gottfried Wilhelm, Freiherr von, 1646-1716.
    Correspondence / G.W. Leibniz and Samuel Clarke ; edited with
an introduction, by Roger Ariew.
        p. cm.
    ISBN 0-87220-524-X (pbk.) — ISBN 0-87220-525-8 (cloth).
    1. Leibniz, Gottfried Wilhelm, Freiherr von, 1646-1716—
Correspondence.   2. Clarke, Samuel, 1675-1729—Correspondence.
3. Philosophers—Germany—Correspondence.   4. Philosophers—
England—Correspondence.   5. Natural theology—Early works to
1900.   6. Newton, Isaac, Sir, 1642-1727.   I. Clarke, Samuel.
II. Ariew, Roger.   III. Title.

B2597 .A4   2000
193—dc21   99-052339
                                                    CIP

ISBN-13: 978-0-87220-525-3 (cloth)
ISBN-13: 978-0-87220-524-6 (pbk.)

Contents

Abbreviations

AG   G. W. Leibniz, *Philosophical Essays*, eds. and trans. Roger Ariew and Daniel Garber (Indianapolis: Hackett Publishing Company, 1989)

G   G. W. Leibniz, *Die philosophischen Schriften*, ed. C. I. Gerhardt, 7 vols. (Berlin, 1875–1890; reprint ed. Hildesheim: Georg Olms, 1978)

GM   G. W. Leibniz, *Mathematische Schriften*, ed. C. I. Gerhardt, 7 vols. (Berlin, 1849–1855; reprint ed. Hildesheim: Georg Olms, 1962)

H   G. W. Leibniz, *Theodicy*, trans. E. M. Huggard (La Salle, IL: Open Court, 1985)

K   *Die Werke von Leibniz*, ed. O. Klopp, 11 vols. (Hanover, 1864–1884; reprint ed. Hildesheim: Olms, 1973)

L   G. W. Leibniz, *Philosophical Papers and Letters*, ed. and trans. L. Loemker (Dordrecht: Reidel, 1969)

Introduction

Leibniz, Caroline, Newton, and Clarke

In November of 1715, Gottfried Wilhelm Leibniz, the elderly librarian, historian, and counselor to the House of Hanover in Lower Saxony, wrote a letter to Caroline, Princess of Wales, cautioning her about the odd cosmological-theological views of Sir Isaac Newton and his followers. This would seem an unusual event in international relations except that Leibniz had a long-standing relationship with Caroline, who was married to Georg August. The latter was Prince of Wales, Elector Prince of Hanover, and son of Leibniz's employer, Georg Ludwig, Elector of Hanover[1] who, from 1714 on, was George I, King of Great Britain and Ireland. Caroline became Queen Consort in 1727 when Georg August ascended to the throne of England as George II;[2] she was the third of three royal women who had befriended Leibniz.[3] The whole court of Hanover had moved to London in 1714. However, Leibniz was not welcome there. Georg Ludwig had refused his request to join the royal family in England. The official reason was that he was to stay in Hanover until the history of the House of Hanover, which he was commissioned to write, was closer to completion.[4] By 1714 there was great hostility at the

---

1. Elector Georg Ludwig was the third of Leibniz's employers in Hanover (from 1698 to Leibniz's death in 1716), the first having been Duke Johann Freidrich who first retained Leibniz (from 1676 to 1679) and the second his brother Duke, then Elector, Ernst August (Leibniz's employer from 1679 to 1698 and Georg Ludwig's father).

2. Caroline was the mother of Frederick Louis, Prince of Wales, and thus grandmother of George III, "Old King George" of the American Revolution. For more on Caroline and the context for the correspondence, see Domenico Bertoloni Meli, "Caroline, Leibniz, and Clarke," *Journal of the History of Ideas* 60 (1999): 469–86.

3. Including Georg Ludwig's sister Sophia Charlotte, Electress of Brandenburg, then Queen of Prussia, and his mother Sophia, Electress of Hanover.

4. Ernst August had asked Leibniz to write a history of the House of Hanover in the 1680s. Leibniz took on the task with his customary zeal and optimism, that is, he took on much more than he could reasonably accomplish. The only finished manuscript of the history he left behind was its first volume, *Protogaea*, a treatise on natural history or geology. Leibniz intended to preface his history with a dissertation on the state of Germany as it was prior to all histories, taking as evidence the natural monuments, shells petrified in earth, and stones with the imprint of fish or plants. He contemplated continuing his history by treating the oldest known

court to the then elderly counselor. He was often a subject of ridicule, treated as an old fossil, with his enormous black wig and once fashionable ornate clothes. The court may have been unhappy with his failure to finish the history of the House of Hanover,[5] but it was also surely embarrassed by the protracted debate between him and Newton over the discovery of the calculus, which had taken on decidedly nationalistic overtones.[6]

Admittedly, the debate about the priority of the invention of the calculus was not the only controversy of the final period of Leibniz's life, but it was certainly the most bitter. The first public blow in the dispute was probably delivered by Fatio de Dullier, who wrote an article in 1697 attributing the discovery to Newton and attacking Leibniz. The feud

---

people, then the different peoples that succeeded one another, their languages, and the mixtures of these languages, to the extent that they can be judged by etymologies. The origins of the House would have begun with Charlemagne and continued with the Emperors descended from him and with the five Emperors of the House of Brunswick, encompassing the ancient history of Saxony through the House of Witikind, of Upper Germany through the House of the Guelfs, and of Lombardy through the Houses of the Dukes and Marquis of Tuscany and Liguria, thus tracing the descent of the Princes of Brunswick. After these origins would have come the genealogy of the House of the Guelfs, with a short history up to the seventeenth century; the genealogy would have been accompanied by those of the other great Houses, including the House of the Ghibellines, ancient and modern Austria, and Bavaria. To accomplish his design and to amass sufficient materials, Leibniz scoured the whole of Germany, visited ancient abbeys, searched town archives, and examined tombs and other antiquities. Although he never completed his history, we should not think that he balked at the project; one cannot look upon the masses of corollary materials he did publish and think that he was not committed to it. He left behind enough materials that G. H. Pertz, a Hanover librarian and editor of Leibniz's works, was able to put it all together and finally publish the history in four fat volumes during the nineteenth century.

5. And perhaps other failures: Leibniz took on a wide variety of tasks for the court at Hanover. One of his initial tasks was as mining engineer, supervising the draining of the silver mines in the Harz mountains. His plan was to use the power of air, for which he designed windmills, gearing mechanisms, and suction pumps. It all ended up in defeat, Leibniz believing that he was undermined by various lower administrators and workers who feared that the technology would cost them their jobs.

6. It does not take much imagination to see that the Court of Hanover might have had divided loyalties between their German past and their English future; it is clear that they wanted to look more English as they became the Royal Court. Leibniz, as a German disputant in a controversy with the English Newtonians, would not have fitted well into their plans. For a discussion of such issues, see E. J. Aiton, *Leibniz: A Biography* (Bristol: A. Hilger, 1985).

simmered, and in 1711 Leibniz complained to the Royal Society about an accusation by John Keill, another Newtonian, that Leibniz had stolen Newton's calculus.[7] In 1712 the Society declared that Leibniz did not know anything of differential calculus before Newton revealed it to him in a letter of 1672; that Newton invented the calculus in 1669, fifteen years before Leibniz published his version of it in the *Acta Eruditorum* of Leipzig; and that, consequently, Keill had not slandered Leibniz. The Society made its findings public in its *Commercium Epistolicum de Analysi promota* (mostly composed by Newton, as we now understand). The episode obviously had many repercussions up to Leibniz's death four years later. Perhaps the only charitable thing one could say about it is that it provides a glimpse into the workings of the Royal Society at the start of the eighteenth century and illustrates its domination by Newton and the Newtonians.[8]

Newton (1642–1727) was, of course, the foremost mathematician and natural philosopher of the late seventeenth century. He attended Trinity College, Cambridge, was elected Fellow in 1667, and succeeded Isaac Barrow as Lucasian Professor of Mathematics in 1669. Newton's great work, *Philosophiae naturalis principia mathematica* (*The Mathematical Principles of Natural Philosophy,* referred to as the *Principia*), published in 1687 (2nd ed. 1713; 3rd ed. 1726), was a revision and expansion of several treatises he previously composed but did not publish. He was elected President of the Royal Society in 1703 and knighted in 1705, the year after the publication of *Optics*. During his life he engaged in several bitter priority disputes about scientific and mathematical discoveries—for example, with Robert Hooke in 1686–1688 over the inverse square law and, of course, with Leibniz over the calculus. His influence in the history of science is unequaled.[9]

7. Keill had made his accusation of plagiarism in the 1708 *Philosophical Transactions* of the Society. It seems that, for a long time, Leibniz naively believed that Keill had acted without Newton's knowledge.

8. See Mordechai Feingold, "Mathematicians and Naturalists: Isaac Newton and the Nature of the Early Royal Society," in *Isaac Newton's Natural Philosophy*, Jed Buchwald and I. Bernard Cohen, eds. (Cambridge, MA: MIT Press, 2000). For an account of the dispute between Newton and Leibniz on the calculus, see A. Rupert Hall, *Philosophers at War* (Cambridge: Cambridge University Press, 1980).

9. For more on Newton, see Richard W. Westfall, *Never at Rest* (Cambridge: Cambridge University Press, 1980), I. Bernard Cohen, *The Newtonian Revolution* (Cambridge: Cambridge University Press, 1980), or B. J. Dobbs, *The Janus Faces of Genius: The Role of Alchemy in Newton's Thought* (Cambridge: Cambridge University Press, 1991). Two useful collections of Newton's writing in English translation

When Leibniz wrote to Caroline cautioning her about Newton's views, he surely did not expect to elicit a reply from Newton. But by the end of the month, on November 26, 1715, he had received a letter written by Samuel Clarke on behalf of Newton. This resulted in a series of four more letters by Leibniz and four more replies by Clarke, the exchange being cut short by Leibniz's death on November 14, 1716. There is always a lingering question of authorship in Clarke's letters: were they really Clarke's or were they composed by Newton? Clarke was obviously Newton's stand-in, but was he also merely a mouthpiece? Enzio Vailati, the author of a recent commentary on the Leibniz-Clarke correspondence, reviews the arguments both pro and con:

> First, the documentary evidence about Newton's role in the correspondence is scant at best. There are neither drafts of Clarke's letters to Leibniz by Newton nor letters between Clarke and Newton that might help in assessing the latter's role in the correspondence. Since Clarke was Newton's parish priest at St. James, Picadilly, they were neighbors, which rendered epistolary exchanges unlikely. . . . We know that Newton played some indirect role in the correspondence. There is a copy in Newton's hand of the postscript on atoms and void to Clarke's fourth letter, and almost certainly Clarke consulted some of his papers in drafting the physical arguments that make up much of the notes in his fifth letter; but whether Newton played a direct role, and if so what its extent and depth were, is unclear at best.[10]

The author goes on to state that Clarke's views coincided with Newton's and that Newton's influence on Clarke was great, but that "all the philosophical positions and most of the arguments Clarke aired in the correspondence had appeared in his 1705–1706 Boyle Lectures, in previous epistolary exchanges with Collins (1707–1708) and Butler (1714–1715), and in philosophical sermons."[11] All of that is surely right, and Vailati's emphasis in reestablishing Clarke as a philosopher who should be studied seriously is certainly welcome. Still, there is no doubt that Clarke was Newton's agent and that he would not have written anything that he knew

---

are *Newton's Philosophy of Nature, Selections from His Writings*, H. S. Thayer, ed. (New York: Hafner Press, 1953) and *Newton: Texts, Backgrounds, Commentaries*, I. Bernard Cohen and Richard S. Westfall, eds. (New York: W. W. Norton, 1995). There is a new translation of Newton's *Principia* by I. Bernard Cohen and Anne Whitman, *The Principia: Mathematical Principles of Natural Philosophy*, (Berkeley: University of California Press,1999).

   10. Enzio Vailati, *Leibniz and Clarke, A Study of Their Correspondence* (Oxford: Oxford University Press, 1997), p. 4.

   11. Vailati, *Leibniz and Clarke*, pp. 4–5.

was not in keeping with Newton's views. The relationship between Clarke and Newton was too close to think of Clarke as independent. That was also how Caroline saw it. In the letter she wrote to Leibniz on January 10, 1716, enclosed with Clarke's *Second Replies*, she said:

> I enclose a reply to your paper; I considered very carefully the replies made on both sides. I do not know whether the bias I have for your merit makes me partial, but I find all his replies are rather words than what could be called replies. You are right about the author of the reply; they are not written without the advice of Sir Newton, whom I should like to be reconciled with you. I do not know if you will consent, but the Abbé Conti and myself have made ourselves mediators; it would be a great pity if two such great men as you and he were to be estranged by misunderstandings.[12]

Ironically, Leibniz had previously asked about the possibility of translating the *Theodicy* into English and Caroline had written to him on November 14, 1715, saying: "I have talked today with the Bishop of Lincoln about the translation of your *Theodicy*; he assures me that there is no one capable of doing it except Dr. Clarke, whose books I sent you by Oeynhausen. He is a close friend of Sir Newton."[13] But less than two weeks later, in the letter in which she enclosed Clarke's *First Reply*, Caroline said:

> I hope you received the books I sent you. Send me, please, your opinion on Dr. Clarke's works, which I think have considerable merit, although not comparable to your *Theodicy*. . . . We are thinking seriously of getting your *Theodicy* translated; but we are looking for a good translator. Dr. Clarke is too opposed to your opinions to do it; he would certainly be the most suitable person of all, but he is too much of Sir Isaac Newton's opinion and I am myself engaged in a dispute with him.[14]

Caroline's opinion of Clarke was clearly correct: he was an excellent translator of philosophy and science but he was too much of the Newtonian.

Samuel Clarke (1675–1729) was educated at Gonville and Caius College, Cambridge, receiving his B.A. in 1695. It was said that he was one of the first to master Newton's *Principia*. In 1697 he translated into Latin the *Traité de physique* of the Cartesian Jacques Rohault, adding extensive footnotes "correcting" Descartes by incorporating Newtonian principles. It became the standard physics textbook in English schools and thereby the conduit through which Newtonian principles were taught—it was

12. K XI, 71.
13. K XI, 50.
14. K XI, 52.

itself translated into English, footnotes and all, by John Clarke (1682–1757) in 1723. Samuel Clarke also published several theological works and sermons and was involved in various theological disputes (including the one with Henry Dodwell over the immortality of the soul mentioned in the correspondence). He gave the Boyle lectures in 1704 and 1705. In 1706 he translated Newton's *Optics* into Latin. But perhaps he is best known now for his correspondence with Leibniz, in which he and Leibniz had a wide-ranging discussion of the nature of God, human souls, free will and indifference of choice, space and time, the vacuum, miracles, and matter and force.

These philosophical topics have always been important, but they took on an even greater significance in the seventeenth century, when philosophers had to reconsider their fundamental doctrines in the light of the scientific revolution that was taking place. New scientific and philosophical doctrines had emerged, posing a challenge to the Aristotelian (or scholastic) philosophy, which had dominated European thought ever since the thirteenth century when the majority of the Aristotelian corpus was rediscovered, translated from Greek and Arabic into Latin, and made compatible with Christian doctrine. The substantial forms and primary matter of the scholastics were giving way to a new mechanistic world of geometrical bodies, corpuscles, or atoms in motion. Old problems that seemed to have been resolved within a scholastic framework were raised again with new urgency. Leibniz, of course, was a major contributor to this intellectual movement, which defined the modern world.

Leibniz (1646–1716) attended the universities of Leipzig (1661–1666) and Altdorf (1666–1667), graduating with degrees in law and philosophy. Invited to join the faculty at Altdorf, he chose instead to enter the service of the Elector of Mainz. In 1672 he was sent on diplomatic business to Paris. While in Paris, he read and copied René Descartes's manuscripts and sought out proponents of the new philosophy, including Antoine Arnauld and Nicholas Malebranche; his own later work was often precipitated by the correspondence he maintained with them. He traveled to London and met members of the Royal Society (Henry Oldenburg and Robert Boyle, among others, though not Newton). Leibniz returned to Germany, in 1676, in the service of the court of Hanover, where he resided until his death. His literary output was massive, but he did not publish much of what he wrote. Among his unpublished manuscripts were such important works as "Discourse on Metaphysics" (1686), *Dynamics* (1689–1691), and "Monadology" (1714). In 1705 he finished his *New Essays on Human Understanding,* a book-length commentary on John Locke's *Essay* but did not issue the work. He usually wrote essays, small treatises, and letters to learned correspondents. With the rise of intellectual journals in the second half of the seventeenth century, he had a ready means of disseminating his thought. He did publish several significant philosophical articles: "New System of Nature" (*Journal des Scavants*, 1695), "Specimen of Dynamics" (*Acta Eruditorum*, 1695), and "On Nature Itself" (*Acta Eruditorum*, 1698). Ultimately, he published a book-length volume, *Theodicy* (1710), though it is a rather loosely structured work, consisting largely of responses to Pierre Bayle's skepticism. Leibniz maintained an extensive circle of correspondents.[15]

The correspondence with Clarke took place during Leibniz's last few years; as such, the doctrines it contains resemble those of the *Theodicy* and "Monadology." In the exchange Leibniz is especially concerned to defend the principle of sufficient reason as the basis for contingent truths, as opposed to the principle of contradiction, which he asserts is the foundation for necessary truths.[16] He also defends a number of his characteristic theses: small perceptions which we do not consciously perceive, pre-established harmony between the soul and the body, and especially the identity of indiscernibles.[17] According to Leibniz, the thesis of the identity of indiscernibles would "put an end to such doctrines as the empty tablets of the soul, a soul without thought, a substance without action, void space, atoms, and even particles in matter not actually divided, complete uniformity in a part of time, place, or matter . . . and a thousand other fictions of philosophers which arise from their incomplete notions"[18]—doctrines which he disputed with Newton and Clarke.

15. There are a number of collections of Leibniz's philosophical essays as well as editions of the *Theodicy* and *New Essays* in English translation (see the Abbreviations). For more on Leibniz, see: C. D. Broad, *Leibniz: An Introduction* (Cambridge: Cambridge University Press, 1975); Stuart Brown, *Leibniz* (Minneapolis: University of Minnesota Press, 1984); Catherine Wilson, *Leibniz's Metaphysics: A Historical and Comparative Study* (Princeton: Princeton University Press, 1989); Robert Sleigh, *Leibniz and Arnauld* (New Haven: Yale University Press, 1990); Donald Rutherford, *Leibniz and the Rational Order of Nature* (Cambridge: Cambridge University Press, 1995); Nicholas Jolley, ed., *The Cambridge Companion to Leibniz* (Cambridge: Cambridge University Press, 1995).

16. Principle of sufficient reason: "that nothing is without a sufficient reason why it is, and why it is thus rather than otherwise"; principle of contradiction: "that a proposition cannot be true and false at the same time, and that therefore A is A and cannot be not A." See "Monadology," sec. 31–3, AG 217.

17. "Two individual things cannot be perfectly alike and must always differ in something over and above number."

18. AG 297.

Editor's Note

Clarke accomplished most of the work for this edition. In 1717 he published the correspondence between him and Leibniz as *A Collection of Papers which passed between the late Mr. Leibnitz and Dr. Clarke in the years 1715 and 1716 relating to the Principles of Natural Philosophy and Religion*, in English and French on facing pages, with Leibniz's letters translated into English by him. He even translated and incorporated into the edition some passages from Leibniz's (French and Latin) works that would illuminate their exchanges. I have simply modernized Clarke's translation for an American audience. I also checked his translation against Leibniz's original language. Most of the modifications I made were minor, a result of changing standards of spelling and punctuation. Other modifications, also minor, had to do with various words we consider archaic; when Leibniz talks about *le mercure* and *l'aimant*, Clarke's translations are "quicksilver" and "the lodestone," whereas we would say "mercury" and "the magnet." Some of the revisions had to do with ambiguous terms in Enlightenment English. Clarke uses the term *want* to mean need or lack, as in Leibniz's "principle of the want of a sufficient reason" or Newton's "until this system wants a reformation" and his own "for want of gravity." We generally restrict *want* to what agents do. I attempted to dispel this ambiguity, which does not occur in Leibniz's French. Leibniz's principle is that of a *besoin d'une raison suffisante*, or of a "need for a sufficient reason." And when Clarke translates him as saying "for want of knowledge," he is translating *faute de connaissance*, or "for lack of knowledge." There is a similar ambiguity with the English verb *pretend*, which can mean either claim or feign. Again, Leibniz's French is not ambiguous; he says *je pretends les avoir établis*—"I claim"—not Clarke's "I pretend"—"to have established them," and *On me l'avoit même accordé, ou fait semblant de l'accorder*—"The author granted it or pretended to grant it." Similar things may be said about *alleguer*, which does not have the connotation that *allege* has in a non-legal context, but is more like advance or adduce. Perhaps the only major revision I made was to sort out Clarke's vocabulary as to the word *perceive*, which he uses to translate indifferently Leibniz's *sentir*, *percevoir*, *appercevoir* and *representer*. The first pair I left as "perceive," but translated *appercevoir* as "consciously perceive" and *representer* as "represent"; see my note to sec. 4 of Leibniz's *Second Letter*. Finally, other than this brief Introduction, I added a few explanatory notes and an appendix with some portions of Newton's works that may be helpful toward understanding the exchanges, especially as they are often referred to by Clarke.

I wish to thank David Bruzina, for assisting me in establishing the text and checking it against Clarke's published version, and Gregory Brown, for the chronological table he prepared in 1994 of Leibniz and royalty (it came in handy when I was trying to remember all the various relations in the House of Hanover). I also wish to thank Daniel Garber, Mordechai Feingold, and Marjorie Grene for their many useful suggestions in the preparation of this edition.

Clarke's Introduction

To Her Royal Highness the Princess of Wales

Madam,

As the following letters were at first written by your command and had afterwards the honor of being transmitted several times through Your Royal Highness' hands, so the principal encouragement upon which they now presume to appear in public is the permission they have of coming forth under the protection of so illustrious a name.

The late learned Mr. Leibniz understood well how great an honor and reputation it would be to him to have his arguments approved by a person of Your Royal Highness' character. But the same steady impartiality and unalterable love of truth, the same constant readiness to hear and to submit to reason, always so conspicuous, always shining forth so brightly in Your Royal Highness' conduct—which justly made him desirous to exert in these papers his utmost skill in defending his opinions—was at the same time an equal encouragement, to those who thought him in error, to endeavor to prove that his opinions could not be defended.

The occasion of his giving your Royal Highness the trouble of his first letter, he declares to be his having entertained some suspicions that the foundations of natural religion were in danger of being hurt by Sir Isaac Newton's philosophy. It appeared to me, on the contrary, a most certain and evident truth that, from the earliest antiquity to this day, the foundations of natural religion had never been so deeply and so firmly laid as in the mathematical and experimental philosophy of that great man. And Your Royal Highness' singular exactness in searching after truth and earnest concern for everything of real consequence to religion could not permit those suspicions, which had been suggested by a gentleman of such eminent note in the learned world as Mr. Leibniz was, to remain unanswered.

Christianity presupposes the truth of natural religion. Whatever subverts natural religion does consequently much more subvert Christianity, and whatever tends to confirm natural religion is proportionately of service to the true interest of the Christian. Natural philosophy, therefore, insofar as it affects religion by determining questions concerning liberty and fate, concerning the extent of the powers of matter and motion and the proofs from phenomena of God's continual government of the world, is of very great importance. It is of singular use to understand rightly and distinguish carefully from hypotheses or mere suppositions the true and certain consequences of experimental and mathematical philosophy, which do, with wonderful strength and advantage to all such as are capable of apprehending them, confirm, establish, and vindicate against all objections those great and fundamental truths of natural religion, which the wisdom of providence has at the same time universally implanted, in some degree, in the minds of persons even of the meanest capacities not qualified to examine demonstrative proofs.

It is with the highest pleasure and satisfaction that the following papers on so important a subject are laid before a Princess, who, to an inimitable sweetness of temper, candor, and affability toward all, has joined not only an impartial love of truth and a desire for promoting learning in general, but has herself also attained to a very particular and uncommon degree of knowledge, even in matters of the nicest and most abstract speculation, and whose sacred and always unshaken regard to the interest of sincere and uncorrupt religion made her the delight of all good Protestants abroad, and by a just fame filled the hearts of all true Britons at home with an expectation beforehand, which, great as it was, is fully answered by what they now see and are blessed with.

By the Protestant Succession in the illustrious house of Hanover having taken place, this nation has now, with the blessing of God, a certain prospect (if our own vices and follies do not prevent it) of seeing government actually administered, according to the design and end for which it was instituted by providence, with no other view than that of the public good, the general welfare and happiness of mankind. We have a prospect of seeing the true liberty of a brave and loyal people, firmly secured, established, and regulated by laws equally advantageous both to the crown and subject; of seeing learning and knowledge encouraged and promoted, in opposition to all kinds of ignorance and blindness; and (which is the glory of all) of seeing the true Christian temper and spirit of religion effectively prevail, both against atheism and infidelity on the one hand, which take off from men all obligations of doing what is right, and against superstition and bigotry on the other hand, which lay upon men the strongest obligations to do the greatest wrongs.

What views and expectations less than these can a nation reasonably entertain, when it beholds a King firmly settled upon the throne of a wisely limited monarchy, whose will, when without limitation always showed a greater love of justice than of power, and never took pleasure in acting otherwise than according to the most perfect laws of reason and equity? When it sees a succession of the same blessings continued, in a Prince, whose noble openness of mind and generous warmth of zeal for the preservation of the Protestant religion and the laws and liberties of these kingdoms, make him every day more and more beloved as he is more known? And when these glorious hopes open still further into an unbounded prospect in a numerous royal offspring? Through whom, that the just and equitable temper of the grandfather, the noble zeal and spirit of the father, the affability, goodness, and judicious exactness of the mother, may, with glory to themselves and with the happiest influences both on these and foreign countries, descend to all succeeding generations; to the establishment of universal peace, of truth and right among men; and to the entire rooting out that greatest enemy of Christian religion, the spirit of Popery both among Romanists and Protestants, and that Your Royal Highness may yourself live long, to continue a blessing to these nations, to see truth and virtue flourish in your own days, and to be a great instrument under the direction of providence in laying a foundation for the highest happiness of the public in times to come, is the prayer of, Madam, Your Royal Highness' most humble and most obedient servant, Samuel Clarke.

Advertisement to the Reader

The reader will be pleased to observe,

1. That the following letters are all printed exactly as they were written, without adding, diminishing, or altering a word. Only the marginal notes and the Appendix were added.[1]

2. That the translation is made with great exactness to prevent any misrepresentation of Leibniz's sense.

3. That the numbers of sections in each of Clarke's letters refer respectively to the numbers or sentences of each of Leibniz's immediately preceding letters.[2]

---

1. As Clarke states, he inserted an appendix with passages from Leibniz's works and added a large number of marginal references. We have reproduced the appendix (as Appendix A) and incorporated the marginal references as footnotes or (in the case of the section references from Clarke's *Fifth Reply*) in the text itself.

2. Clarke added the section numbers to Leibniz's *First* and *Second Letters* and to his own *First* and *Second Replies*.

Correspondence

Leibniz's First Letter, Being an Extract of a Letter Written in November, 1715[3]

1. Natural religion itself seems to decay [in England] very much. Many will have human souls to be material; others make God himself a corporeal being.

2. Mr. Locke and his followers are uncertain at least whether the soul is not material and naturally perishable.[4]

3. Sir Isaac Newton says that space is an organ which God makes use of to perceive things by. But if God stands in need of any organ to perceive things by, it will follow that they do not depend altogether on him, nor were produced by him.

4. Sir Isaac Newton and his followers also have a very odd opinion concerning the work of God. According to their doctrine, God Almighty needs to wind up his watch from time to time,[5] otherwise it would cease to move. He did not, it seems, have sufficient foresight to make it a perpetual motion. No, the machine of God's making is so imperfect, according to these gentlemen, that he is obliged to clean it now and then by an extraordinary concourse, and even to mend it, as a clockmaker mends his work; he must consequently be so much the more unskillful a workman as he is more often obliged to mend his work and to set it right. According to my opinion, the same force[6] and vigor always remains in the world and only passes from one part of matter to another in agreement with the laws of nature and the beautiful pre-established order. And I hold that when God works miracles, he does not do it in order to supply the needs of nature, but those of grace. Whoever thinks otherwise, must necessarily have a very mean notion of the wisdom and power of God.

---

3. To Caroline, Princess of Wales.

4. See Locke, *Essay Concerning Human Understanding* IV, 3.6 and *First Letter to Stillingfleet*. See also Leibniz's Preface to the *New Essays*, AG 291–306, esp. pp. 300 et seq.

5. According to Clarke, Leibniz is alluding to a passage in Newton's *Optics*, Query 31 ending with: "which will be apt to increase, until this system needs a reformation." See Appendix B, no. 3.

6. Clarke directs the reader to his long footnote about force at the end of the *Fifth Reply*, concerning sec. 93–5. He also refers to Leibniz's writings, Appendix A, no. 2, and to Leibniz's *Fifth Letter*, sec. 87 and 91.

Clarke's First Reply[7]

1. That there are some in England as well as in other countries who deny or very much corrupt even natural religion itself is very true and much to be lamented. But (next to the vicious affections of men) this is to be principally ascribed to the false philosophy of the materialists, to which the mathematical principles of philosophy are the most directly repugnant. That some make the souls of men, and others even God himself, to be a corporeal being is also very true, but those who do so are the great enemies of the mathematical principles of philosophy; these principles, and these alone, prove matter or body to be the smallest and most inconsiderable part of the universe.

2. That Mr. Locke doubted whether the soul was immaterial or not may justly be suspected from some parts of his writings, but in this he has been followed only by some materialists, enemies of the mathematical principles of philosophy, who approve little or nothing in Mr. Locke's writings but his errors.

3. Sir Isaac Newton does not say that space is the organ which God makes use of to perceive things by, nor that he has need of any medium at all by which to perceive things, but on the contrary that he, being omnipresent, perceives all things by his immediate presence to them in all space, wherever they are, without the intervention or assistance of any organ or medium whatsoever. In order to make this more intelligible, he illustrates it by a similitude: that as the mind of man, by its immediate presence to the pictures or images of things formed in the brain by the means of the organs of sensation, sees those pictures as if they were the things themselves, so God sees all things by his immediate presence to them, given that he is actually present to the things themselves, to all things in the universe, as the mind of man is present to all the pictures of things formed in his brain. Sir Isaac Newton considers the brain and organs of sensation as the means by which those pictures are formed, but not as the means by which the mind sees or perceives those pictures when they are so formed. And he does not consider things in the universe as if they were pictures formed by certain means or organs, but as real things formed by God himself and seen by him in all places wherever they are, without the intervention of any medium at all. And this similitude is all that he means when he supposes infinite space to be (as it were) the *sensorium* of the omnipresent Being.[8]

7. November 26, 1715.

8. Clarke refers to the following passage from Newton's *Optics*, Query 28: "Is not the sensorium of animals the place where the sensitive substance is present,

4. The reason why, among men, an artificer is justly esteemed so much the more skillful, as the machine of his composing will continue longer to move regularly without any further interposition of the workman, is because the skill of all human artificers consists only in composing, adjusting, or putting together certain movements, the principles of whose motion are altogether independent of the artificer: such are weights and springs and the like, whose forces are not made but only adjusted by the workman. But with regard to God the case is quite different, because he not only composes or puts things together, but is himself the author and continual preserver of their original forces or moving powers; and consequently it is not a diminution, but the true glory of his workmanship, that nothing is done without his continual government and inspection. The notion of the world's being a great machine, going on without the interposition of God as a clock continues to go without the assistance of a clockmaker, is the notion of materialism and fate, and tends (under pretence of making God a *supramundane intelligence*)[9] to exclude providence and God's government in reality out of the world. And by the same reason that a philosopher can represent all things going on from the beginning of the creation without any government or interposition of providence, a skeptic will easily argue still farther backwards and suppose that things have from eternity gone on (as they now do) without any true creation or original author at all, but only what such arguers call all-wise and eternal nature. If a king had a kingdom in which all things would continually go on without his government or interposition, or without his attending to and ordering what is done in the kingdom, it would be to him merely a nominal kingdom, nor would he in reality deserve at all the title of king or governor. And as those men who claim that in an earthly government things may go on perfectly well without the king himself ordering or disposing of anything may reasonably be suspected that they would like very well to set the king aside, so whoever contends that the course of the world can go on without the continual direction of God, the Supreme Governor, his doctrine does in effect tend to exclude God out of the world.

---

and to which the sensible species of things are carried by the nerves and brain, that they may be perceived there, as being present to the sensitive substance? And do not the phenomena of nature show that there is an incorporeal, living, intelligent, omnipresent being who, in the infinite space, which is as it were his sensorium (or place of perception), sees and discerns the very things themselves in the most intimate and thorough manner, and comprehends them as entirely and immediately present within himself—of these things the sensitive and thinking substance that is in us perceives and views, in its little sensorium, nothing but the images carried there by the organs of the senses?"

9. See Appendix A, no. 1.

Leibniz's Second Letter, Being an Answer to Clarke's First Reply[10]

1. It is rightly observed in the paper delivered to the Princess of Wales, which Her Royal Highness has been pleased to communicate to me, that next to corruption of manners, the principles of the materialists do very much contribute to keep up impiety. But I believe that one has no reason to add that the mathematical principles of philosophy are opposite to those of the materialists. On the contrary, they are the same, only with this difference—that the materialists, in imitation of Democritus, Epicurus, and Hobbes, confine themselves altogether to mathematical principles and admit only bodies, whereas the Christian mathematicians also admit immaterial substances. For this reason, not mathematical principles (according to the usual sense of that word) but *metaphysical principles* ought to be opposed to those of the materialists. Pythagoras, Plato, and Aristotle in some measure had a knowledge of these principles, but I claim to have established them demonstratively in my *Theodicy*, though I have done it in a popular manner. The great foundation of mathematics is the *principle of contradiction or identity*, that is, that a proposition cannot be true and false at the same time, and that therefore A is A and cannot be not A. This single principle is sufficient to demonstrate every part of arithmetic and geometry, that is, all mathematical principles. But in order to proceed from mathematics to natural philosophy, another principle is required, as I have observed in my *Theodicy*; I mean the *principle of sufficient reason*, namely, that nothing happens without a reason why it should be so rather than otherwise. And therefore Archimedes, being desirous to proceed from mathematics to natural philosophy, in his book *De aequilibrio,* was obliged to make use of a particular case of the great principle of sufficient reason. He takes it for granted that if there is a balance in which everything is alike on both sides,[11] and if equal weights are hung on the two ends of that balance, the whole will be at rest. That is because no reason can be given why one side should weigh down rather than the other.[12] Now, by that single principle, namely, that there ought to be a sufficient reason why things should be so and not otherwise, one may demonstrate the being of God and all the other parts of metaphysics or natural theology and even, in some measure, those principles of natural philosophy that are independent of mathematics; I mean the dynamic principles or the principles of force.[13]

10. End of December, 1715.
11. See Appendix A, no. 3.
12. See Archimedes, *On the Equilibrium of Planes*, book I, postulate 1.
13. See Appendix A, no. 2.

2. The author proceeds and says that according to the *mathematical principles*, that is, according to Sir Isaac Newton's philosophy (for *mathematical principles* determine nothing in the present case), matter is the most inconsiderable part of the universe. The reason is because he admits empty space besides matter and because, according to his notions, matter fills up only a very small part of space. But Democritus and Epicurus maintained the same thing; they differed from Sir Isaac Newton only as to the quantity of matter, and perhaps they believed there was more matter in the world than Sir Isaac Newton will allow; in this I think their opinion ought to be preferred, for the more matter there is, the more God has occasion to exercise his wisdom and power. This is one reason, among others, why I maintain that there is no vacuum at all.

3. I find, in express words in the Appendix to Sir Isaac Newton's *Optics*,[14] that space is the *sensorium* of God. But the word *sensorium* has always signified the organ of sensation. He and his friends may now, if they think fit, explain themselves quite otherwise; I shall not be against it.

4. The author supposes that the presence of the soul is sufficient to make it consciously perceive[15] what passes in the brain. But this is the very thing that Father Malebranche and all the Cartesians deny; and they rightly deny it. More is required besides bare presence to enable one thing to represent[16] what passes in another. Some communication that may be explained, some sort of influence [or things in common or common cause][17] is required for this purpose. Space, according to Sir Isaac Newton, is intimately present to the body contained in it and commensurate with it. Does it follow from this that space consciously perceives what

14. See the footnote to Clarke's *First Reply*, sec. 3.

15. Clark's translation has "perceive" for Leibniz's *appercevoir*. The latter is a technical term in Leibniz's philosophy meaning something like "consciously perceive" (which we have chosen to use)—for example, "Monadology," sec. 14, AG 214–5: "The passing state which involves and represents a multitude in the unity or in the simple substance is nothing other than what one calls *perception*, which should be distinguished from apperception, or consciousness, as will be evident in what follows. This is where the Cartesians have failed badly, since they took no account of the perceptions that we do not consciously perceive. This is also what made them believe that minds alone are monads and that there are no animal souls or other entelechies. With the common people, they have confused a long stupor with death, properly speaking, which made them fall again into the Scholastic prejudice of completely separated souls, and they have even confirmed unsound minds in the belief in the mortality of souls."

16. Clark's translation has "perceive" again, though this time it is for Leibniz's *representer*.

17. The bracketed fragment is missing in Clarke's translation.

passes in a body and remembers it when that body is gone away? Besides, the soul being indivisible, its immediate presence, which may be imagined in the body, would only be in one point. How then could it consciously perceive what happens out of that point? I claim to be the first who has shown how the soul consciously perceives what passes in the body.[18]

5. The reason why God consciously perceives everything is not his bare presence, but also his operation. It is because he preserves things by an action that continually produces whatever is good and perfect in them. But the soul having no immediate influence over the body,[19] nor the body over the soul, their mutual correspondence cannot be explained by their being present to each other.

6. The true and principal reason why we commend a machine is rather based on the effects of the machine than on its cause. We do not inquire so much about the power of the artist as we do about his skill in his workmanship. And therefore the reason advanced by the author for extolling the machine of God's making, based on his having made it entirely without borrowing any materials from outside—that reason, I say, is not sufficient. It is a mere shift the author has been forced to have recourse to, and the reason why God exceeds any other artisan is not only because he makes the whole, whereas all other artisans must have matter to work on. This excellence in God would be only on the account of power. But God's excellence also arises from another cause, namely, wisdom, by which his machine lasts longer and moves more regularly than those of any other artisan whatsoever. He who buys a watch does not mind whether the workman made every part of it himself, or whether he got the several parts made by others and only put them together—provided the watch goes right. And if the workman had received from God even the gift of creating the matter of the wheels, yet the buyer of the watch would not be satisfied, unless the workman had also received the gift of putting them well together. In like manner, he who will be pleased with God's workmanship cannot be so without some other reason than that which the author has here advanced.

7. Thus the skill of God must not be inferior to that of a workman; no, it must go infinitely beyond it. The bare production of everything would indeed show the *power* of God, but it would not sufficiently show his *wisdom*. They who maintain the contrary will fall exactly into the error of the materialists and of Spinoza, from whom they profess to differ. They would, in such case, acknowledge power but not sufficient wisdom in the principle of all things.

18. See Appendix A, no. 5.
19. See Appendix A, no. 5.

8. I do not say the material world is a machine or watch that goes without God's interposition, and I have sufficiently insisted that the creation needs to be continually influenced by its creator. But I maintain it to be a watch that goes without needing to be mended by him; otherwise we must say that God revises himself. No, God has foreseen everything. He has provided a remedy for everything beforehand. There is in his works a harmony, a beauty, already pre-established.

9. This opinion does not exclude God's providence or his government of the world; on the contrary, it makes it perfect. A true providence of God requires a perfect foresight. But then it requires, moreover, not only that he should have foreseen everything, but also that he should have provided for everything beforehand with proper remedies; otherwise, he must lack either wisdom to foresee things or power to provide for them. He will be like the God of the Socinians who lives only from day to day, as Mr. Jurieu says.[20] Indeed, God, according to the Socinians, does not so much as foresee inconveniences, whereas the gentlemen I am arguing with, who oblige him to mend his work, say only that he does not provide against them. But this seems to me to be still a very great imperfection. According to this doctrine, God must lack either power or good will.

10. I do not think I can be rightly blamed for saying that God is *intelligentia supramundana*.[21] Will they say that he is *intelligentia mundana*, that is, the soul of the world? I hope not. However, they will do well to take care not to fall into that notion unawares.

11. The comparison of a king, under whose reign everything should go on without his interposition, is by no means to the present purpose, since God continually preserves everything and nothing can subsist without him. His kingdom therefore is not a nominal one. It is just as if one should say that a king who should originally have taken care to have his subjects so well educated, and should, by his care in providing for their subsistence, preserve them so well in their fitness for their several stations and in their good affection toward him, as that he should have no occasion ever to be amending anything among them, would be only a nominal king.

12. To conclude. If God is obliged to mend the course of nature from time to time, it must be done either supernaturally or naturally. If it is done supernaturally, we must have recourse to miracles in order to explain

20. This probably refers to Pierre Jurieu's *Le tableau du Socinianisme* (The Hague, 1690). The Socinians were a Protestant sect, forerunners of Unitarianism, founded by Laelius and Faustus Socinius. One of the Socinian doctrines was that God's foreknowledge was limited to what was necessary and did not apply to the possible.

21. See Appendix A, no. 1.

natural things,[22] which is reducing a hypothesis *ad absurdum*, for everything may easily be accounted for by miracles. But if it is done naturally, then God will not be *intelligentia supramundana*;[23] he will be comprehended under the nature of things, that is, he will be the soul of the world.

Clarke's Second Reply[24]

1. When I said that the mathematical principles of philosophy are opposite to those of the materialists, the meaning was that, whereas materialists suppose the frame of nature to be such as could have arisen from mere mechanical principles of matter and motion, of necessity and fate, the mathematical principles of philosophy show on the contrary that the state of things (the constitution of the sun and planets) is such as could not arise from anything but an intelligent and free cause. As to the propriety of the name: to the extent that metaphysical consequences follow demonstratively from mathematical principles, mathematical principles may (if it is thought fit) be called metaphysical principles.

It is very true that nothing is without a sufficient reason why it is, and why it is thus rather than otherwise. And, therefore, where there is no cause, there can be no effect. But this sufficient reason is often times no other than the mere will of God. There can be no other reason but the mere will of God, for instance, why this particular system of matter should be created in one particular place, and that in another particular place, when (all place being absolutely indifferent to all matter) it would have been exactly the same thing vice versa, supposing the two systems (or the particles) of matter to be alike. And if it could in no case act without a predetermining cause, any more than a balance can move without a preponderating weight, [25] this would tend to take away all power of choosing and to introduce fatality.

2. Many ancient Greeks, who had their philosophy from the Phoenicians and whose philosophy was corrupted by Epicurus, held indeed in general matter and vacuum; but they did not know how to apply those principles to the explanation of the phenomena of nature by mathematics. However small the quantity of matter is, God does not at all have the less subject to exercise his wisdom and power on it, for other things, as well as matter, are equally subjects on which God exercises his power and wisdom. By the same argument it might just as well have been proved that

22. See Appendix A, no. 6.
23. See Appendix A, no. 1.
24. January 10, 1716.
25. See Appendix A, no. 4.

men, or any other particular species of beings, must be infinite in number, lest God should lack subjects on which to exercise his power and wisdom.

3. The word *sensory* does not properly signify the organ, but the place of sensation. The eye, the ear, etc., are organs, but not sensoria. Besides, Sir Isaac Newton does not say that space is the sensory, but that it is, by way of similitude only, "as it were the sensory, etc."[26]

4. It was never supposed that the presence of the soul was sufficient, but only that it is necessary, in order to have perception. Without being present to the images of the things perceived, it could not possibly perceive them, but being present is not sufficient without it being also a living substance. Any inanimate substance, though present, perceives nothing. And a living substance can only perceive where it is present either to the things themselves (as the omnipresent God is to the whole universe) or to the images of things (as the soul of man is in its proper sensory). Nothing can any more act or be acted on where it is not present than it can be where it is not. The soul's being indivisible does not prove it to be present only in a mere point. Space, finite or infinite, is absolutely indivisible, even so much as in thought (to imagine its parts moved from each other is to imagine them moved out of themselves);[27] and yet space is not a mere point.

5. God perceives things, not indeed by his simple presence to them, nor yet by his operation on them, but by his being a living and intelligent, as well as an omnipresent substance. The soul likewise (within its narrow sphere), not by its simple presence, but by its being a living substance, perceives the images to which it is present and which, without being present to them, it could not perceive.

6 and 7. It is very true that the excellence of God's workmanship does not consist in its showing the power only, but in its also showing the wisdom of its author. But then this wisdom of God does not appear in making nature (as an artificer makes a clock) capable of going on without him (for that is impossible, there being no powers of nature independent of God as the powers of weights and springs are independent of men), but the wisdom of God consists in framing originally the perfect and complete idea of a work, which began and continues according to that original perfect idea by the continual uninterrupted exercise of his power and government.

8. The word *correction* or *amendment* is to be understood, not with

26. See the footnote in Clarke's *First Reply*, sec. 3.

27. Clarke refers to Newton, *Principia*, scholium to Definition 8: "As the order of the parts of time is immutable, so also is the order of the parts of space. Suppose these parts to be moved out of their places, and they will be moved (if the expression may be allowed) out of themselves." See Appendix B, no. 1.

regard to God, but only to us. The present frame of the solar system, for instance, according to the present laws of motion, will in time fall into confusion[28] and, perhaps, after that, will be amended or put into a new form. But this amendment is only relative with regard to our conceptions. In reality, and with regard to God, the present frame, and the consequent disorder, and the following renovation, are all equally parts of the design framed in God's original perfect idea. It is in the frame of the world, as in the frame of man's body; the wisdom of God does not consist in making the present frame of either of them eternal, but to last so long as he thought fit.

9. The wisdom and foresight of God do not consist in originally providing remedies that shall of themselves cure the disorders of nature.[29] For in truth and strictness, with regard to God there are no disorders, and consequently no remedies, and indeed no powers of nature at all that can do anything of themselves[30] (as weights and springs work of themselves with regard to men); but the wisdom and foresight of God consist (as has been said) in contriving at once what his power and government is continually putting in actual execution.

10. God is neither a *mundane intelligence,* nor a *supramundane intelligence,*[31] but an omnipresent intelligence, both in and outside the world. He is in all, and through all, as well as above all.

11. If God's conserving all things means his actual operation and government in preserving and continuing the beings, powers, orders, dispositions, and motions of all things, this is all that is contended for. But if his conserving things means no more than a king's creating such subjects as shall be able to act well enough without his intermeddling or ordering anything among them ever after, this is making him indeed a real creator, but only a nominal governor.

12. The argument in this paragraph supposes that whatever God does is supernatural or miraculous, and consequently it tends to exclude all operation of God in the governing and ordering of the natural world. But the truth is, *natural* and *supernatural* are nothing at all different with regard to God, but merely distinctions in our conceptions of things. To cause the sun (or earth) to move regularly is something we call natural. To stop its motion for a day, we call supernatural. But the one is the effect of no greater power than the other; nor is the one with respect to God more

28. See the footnote to Leibniz's *First Letter*, sec. 4.

29. Clarke refers to his "Sermons preached at Mr. Boyle's Lecture," Part I, p. 106 (4th ed.); *Works* (1738; reprint ed. New York: Garland Publishing, 1978), vol. II, p. 566.

30. See Appendix A, no. 2.

31. See Appendix A, no. 1.

or less natural or supernatural than the other. God's being present in or to the world does not make him the soul of the world.[32] A soul is part of a compound, of which body is the other part, and they mutually affect each other as parts of the same whole. But God is present to the world, not as a part, but as a governor, acting on all things, himself acted on by nothing. He is not far from every one of us, for in him we (and all things) live and move and have our beings.

Leibniz's Third Letter, Being an Answer to Clarke's Second Reply[33]

1. According to the usual way of speaking, *mathematical principles* concern only pure mathematics, namely, numbers, figures, arithmetic, geometry. But *metaphysical principles* concern more general notions, such as are cause and effect.

2. The author grants me this important principle, that nothing happens without a sufficient reason why it should be so rather than otherwise. But he grants it only in words and in reality denies it. This shows that he does not fully understand its strength. And therefore he makes use of an instance, which exactly falls in with one of my demonstrations against real absolute space, the idol of some modern Englishmen. I call it an idol, not in a theological sense, but in a philosophical one, as Chancellor Bacon says that there are *idola tribus, idola specus.*[34]

3. These gentlemen maintain, therefore, that space is a real absolute being. But this involves them in great difficulties, for it appears that such a being must necessarily be eternal and infinite. Hence some have believed it to be God himself, or one of his attributes, his immensity. But since space consists of parts, it is not a thing that can belong to God.

4. As for my own opinion, I have said more than once that I hold space to be something purely relative, as time is—that I hold it to be an order of coexistences, as time is an order of successions. For space denotes, in terms of possibility, an order of things that exist at the same time, considered as existing together, without entering into their particular manners of existing. And when many things are seen together, one consciously perceives this order of things among themselves.

5. I have many demonstrations to confute the fancy of those who take

32. Clarke quotes here from the paragraph in Newton's General Scholium to the *Principia* that begins: "This Being governs all things . . ."; see Appendix B, no. 2.

33. February 25, 1716.

34. That is, "idols of the tribe and idols of the cave." See Bacon, *New Organon* I, aphorisms 38–42.

space to be a substance or at least an absolute being. But I shall only use, at present, one demonstration, which the author here gives me occasion to insist upon. I say, then, that if space was an absolute being, something would happen for which it would be impossible that there should be a sufficient reason[35]—which is against my axiom. And I prove it thus: Space is something absolutely uniform, and without the things placed in it, one point of space absolutely does not differ in any respect whatsoever from another point of space. Now from this it follows (supposing space to be something in itself, besides the order of bodies among themselves) that it is impossible there should be a reason why God, preserving the same situations of bodies among themselves, should have placed them in space after one certain particular manner and not otherwise—why everything was not placed the quite contrary way, for instance, by changing east into west. But if space is nothing else but this order or relation, and is nothing at all without bodies but the possibility of placing them, then those two states, the one such as it is now, the other supposed to be the quite contrary way, would not at all differ from one another. Their difference therefore is only to be found in our chimerical supposition of the reality of space in itself. But in truth the one would exactly be the same thing as the other, they being absolutely indiscernible, and consequently there is no room to inquire after a reason for the preference of the one to the other.

6. The case is the same with respect to time. Supposing anyone should ask why God did not create everything a year sooner, and the same person should infer from this that God has done something concerning which it is not possible that there should be a reason why he did it so and not otherwise; the answer is that his inference would be right, if time was anything distinct from things existing in time. For it would be impossible that there should be any reason why things should be applied to such particular instants rather than to others, their succession continuing the same. But then the same argument proves that instants, considered without the things, are nothing at all and that they consist only in the successive order of things; this order remaining the same, one of the two states, namely, that of a supposed anticipation, would not at all differ, nor could be discerned from the other which now is.

7. It appears from what I have said that my axiom has not been well understood and that the author denies it, though he seems to grant it. It is true, he says, that there is nothing without a sufficient reason why it is, and why it is thus rather than otherwise, but he adds that this sufficient reason is often the simple or mere will of God—as when it is asked why matter was not placed elsewhere in space, the same situations of bodies

35. See Appendix A, no. 4.

among themselves being preserved. But this is plainly to maintain that God wills something without any sufficient reason for his will, against the axiom or the general rule of whatever happens. This is falling back into the loose indifference, which I have amply refuted and shown to be absolutely chimerical even in creatures and contrary to the wisdom of God, as if he could operate without acting by reason.

8. The author objects against me that, if we do not admit this simple and pure will, we take away from God the power of choosing and bring in a fatality. But quite the contrary is true. I maintain that God has the power of choosing, since I ground that power on the reason of a choice agreeable to his wisdom. And it is not this fatality (which is only the wisest order of providence) but a blind fatality or necessity void of all wisdom and choice, which we ought to avoid.

9. I had observed that by lessening the quantity of matter, the quantity of objects on which God may exercise his goodness will be lessened. The author answers that instead of matter, there are other things in the void space on which God may exercise his goodness. That may be so, though I do not grant it, for I hold that every created substance is attended with matter. However, let it be so. I answer that more matter was consistent with those same things, and consequently the said objects will be still lessened. The instance of a greater number of men or animals is not to the purpose, for they would fill up place in exclusion of other things.

10. It will be difficult to make me believe that *sensorium* does not, in its usual meaning, signify an organ of sensation. See the words of Rudolphus Goclenius in his *Dictionarium Philosophicum* under *Sensiterium*. "Barbarum Scholasticorum," says he, "qui interdum sunt simiae Graecorum. Hi dicunt *aitheterion*, ex quo illi fecerunt *Sensiterium* pro Sensorio, id est, Organo Sensationis."[36]

11. The mere presence of a substance, even an animated one, is not sufficient for perception. A blind man, and even a man whose thoughts are wandering, does not see. The author must explain how the soul consciously perceives what is outside itself.

12. God is not present to things by situation but by essence; his presence is manifested by his immediate operation. The presence of the soul is

36. Rudolph Goclenius, *Lexicon Philosophicum* (Frankfurt, 1613; reprint ed., Hildesheim: Georg Olms, 1980), p. 1024. Goclenius was a standard reference work for seventeenth-century school philosophers, an alphabetical compendium of standard definitions and distinctions. The passage translates as: "[Sensiterium is] a barbarism due to the scholastics, who sometimes aped the Greeks. The Greeks said aitheterion, from which the scholastics made up *sensiterium*, in place of *sensorium*, that is, the organ of sensation."

of quite another nature. To say that it is diffused all over the body is to make it extended and divisible. To say it is, the whole of it, in every part of the body is to make it divisible of itself.[37] To fix it to a point, to diffuse it all over many points, are only abusive expressions, *idola tribus*.[38]

13. If *active force* should diminish in the universe by the natural laws which God has established, so that there should be need for him to give a new impression in order to restore that force, like an artisan's mending the imperfections of his machine, the disorder would not only be with respect to us, but also with respect to God himself. He might have prevented it and taken better measures to avoid such an inconvenience, and therefore, indeed, he has actually done it.

14. When I said that God has provided remedies beforehand against such disorders, I did not say that God allows disorders to happen and then finds remedies for them, but that he has found a way beforehand to prevent any disorders happening.

15. The author strives in vain to criticize my expression that God is *intelligentia supramundana*.[39] To say that God is above the world is not denying that he is in the world.

16. I never gave any occasion to doubt but that God's conservation is an actual preservation and continuation of the beings, powers, orders, dispositions, and motions of all things, and I think I have perhaps explained it better than many others. But, says the author, "this is all that I contended for." To this I answer, "your humble servant for that, Sir." Our dispute consists in many other things. The question is whether God does not act in the most regular and most perfect manner; whether his machine is liable to disorders, which he is obliged to mend by extraordinary means; whether the will of God can act without reason; whether space is an absolute being; also in what consists the nature of miracles; and many such things, which make a wide difference between us.

17. Theologians will not grant the author's position against me, namely, that there is no difference, with respect to God, between *natural* and *supernatural*; and it will be still less approved by most philosophers. There is a vast difference between these two things, but it plainly appears that it has not been duly considered. That which is supernatural exceeds all the powers of creatures. I shall give an instance which I have often made use of with good success. If God wanted to cause a body to move free in the ether around about a certain fixed center, without any other creature acting on it, I say it could not be done without a miracle, since it

---

37. Clarke had "divided from itself."

38. "Idols of the tribe." See Bacon, *New Organon*, aphorism 41.

39. See Appendix A, no. 1.

cannot be explained by the nature of bodies. For a free body does naturally recede from a curve in the tangent. And therefore I maintain that the attraction of bodies, properly called, is a miraculous thing,[40] since it cannot be explained by the nature of bodies.

Clarke's Third Reply[41]

1. This relates only to the signification of words. The definitions here given may well be allowed, and yet mathematical reasonings may be applied to physical and metaphysical subjects.

2. Undoubtedly nothing is without a sufficient reason why it is rather than not, and why it is thus rather than otherwise. But in things indifferent in their own nature, mere will, without anything external to influence it, is alone that sufficient reason—as in the instance of God's creating or placing any particle of matter in one place rather than in another, when all places are originally alike. And the case is the same, even though space was nothing real but only the mere order of bodies; for still it would be absolutely indifferent, and there could be no other reason but mere will why three equal particles should be placed or ranged in the order a, b, c, rather than in the contrary order. And therefore no argument can be drawn from this indifference of all places to prove that no space is real. For different spaces are really different or distinct one from another, though they are perfectly alike. And there is this evident absurdity in supposing space not to be real but to be merely the order of bodies, that, according to that notion, if the earth and sun and moon had been placed where the most remote fixed stars are now (provided they were placed in the same order and distance they are now with regard one to another) it would not only have been (as this learned author rightly says) *la même chose,* the same thing in effect—which is very true—but it would also follow that they would then have been in the same place too, as they are now—which is an express contradiction.

The ancients did not call all space void of bodies, but only extramundane space, by the name of imaginary space.[42] The meaning of this is not that such space is not real,[43] but only that we are wholly ignorant what

---

40. See Appendix A, no. 8 and the footnote to Clarke's *Fifth Reply,* no. 113.

41. May 15, 1716.

42. Clarke states: "This was occasioned by a passage in the private letter with which Mr. Leibniz's third paper came enclosed." Previous editors of Leibniz's works did not find any such letter among Leibniz's papers.

43. Clarke adds, "Of nothing there are no dimensions, no magnitudes, no quantity, no properties."

kinds of things are in that space. Those writers who, by the word *imaginary*, meant at any time to affirm that space was not real did not thereby prove that it was not real.

3. Space is not a being, an eternal and infinite being, but a property or a consequence of the existence of an infinite and eternal being.[44] Infinite space is immensity, but immensity is not God; and therefore infinite space is not God. Nor is there any difficulty in what is here advanced about space having parts. For infinite space is one, absolutely and essentially indivisible, and to suppose it parted is a contradiction in terms, because there must be space in the partition itself, which is to suppose it parted and yet not parted at the same time.[45] The immensity or omnipresence of God is no more a dividing of his substance into parts than his duration or continuance of existing is a dividing of his existence into parts. There is no difficulty here but what arises from the figurative abuse of the word *parts*.

4. If space was nothing but the order of things coexisting, it would follow that if God should remove in a straight line the whole entire material world, with any speed whatsoever, it would still always continue in the same place, and that nothing would receive any shock upon the most sudden stopping of that motion. And if time was nothing but the order of succession of created things, it would follow that if God had created the world millions of ages sooner than he did, it would not have been created at all the sooner. Further, space and time are quantities, which situation and order are not.

5. The argument in this paragraph is that, because space is uniform or alike, and one part does not differ from another, therefore the bodies created in one place, if they had been created in another place (supposing them to keep the same situation with regard to each other), would still have been created in the same place as before—which is a manifest contradiction. The uniformity of space does indeed prove that there could be no (external) reason why God should create things in one place rather than in another, but does that hinder his own will from being to itself a sufficient reason of acting in any place, when all places are indifferent or alike and there is good reason to act in some place?

6. The same reasoning takes place here as in the foregoing.

7 and 8. Where there is any difference in the nature of things, there the consideration of that difference always determines an intelligent and perfectly wise agent. But when two ways of acting are equally and alike good (as in the instances previously mentioned), to affirm in such case that God

44. Clarke refers to the note from his *Fourth Reply*, sec. 10.
45. Clarke refers to sec. 4 of his *Second Reply*.

cannot act at all,[46] or that it is no perfection in him to be able to act, because he can have no external reason to move him to act one way rather than the other, seems to be a denying God to have in himself any original principle or power of beginning to act, but that he must necessarily be (as it were mechanically) always determined by extrinsic things.

9. I suppose that determinate quantity of matter now in the world is the most convenient for the present frame of nature, or the present state of things, and that a greater (as well as a lesser) quantity of matter would have made the present frame of the world less convenient and consequently would not have been a greater object for God to have exercised his goodness upon.

10. The question is not what Goclenius, but what Sir Isaac Newton means by the word *sensorium*, when the debate is about Sir Isaac Newton's sense,[47] and not about the sense of Goclenius' book. If Goclenius takes the eye or ear or any other organ of sensation to be the sensorium, he is certainly mistaken. But when any writer expressly explains what he means by any term of art, of what use is it in this case to inquire in what different senses perhaps some other writers have sometimes used the same word? Scapula explains it by *domicilium*, the place where the mind resides.[48]

11. The soul of a blind man does not see for this reason, because no images are conveyed to the sensorium where the soul is present (there being some obstruction in the way). How the soul of a seeing man sees the images to which it is present, we do not know, but we are sure it cannot consciously perceive what it is not present to, because nothing can act or be acted on where it is not.

12. God, being omnipresent, is really present to everything essentially and substantially.[49] His presence manifests indeed itself by its operation, but it could not operate if it was not there. The soul is not omnipresent to every part of the body and therefore does not and cannot itself actually operate on every part of the body, but only on the brain or certain nerves and spirits, which, by laws and communications of God's appointing, influence the whole body.

46. See Appendix A, no. 4.

47. Clarke refers to the note in sec. 3 of his *First Reply*.

48. Scapula, *Lexicon Graeco-Latinum* (1639), has "aitheterion: sentienti instrumentum. Nonnulli exp. domicilium sensus [instrument of sensation. Sometimes, place where the sense resides]."

49. Clarke quotes from the end of Newton's General Scholium: "God is omnipresent not only virtually, but substantially, for virtues cannot subsist without substance." See Appendix B, no. 2.

13 and 14. The *active forces,*[50] which are in the universe diminishing
themselves so as to stand in need of new impressions, is no inconvenience,
no disorder, no imperfection in the workmanship of the universe, but is
the consequence of the nature of dependent things. This dependency of
things is not a matter that needs to be rectified. The case of a human
workman making a machine is quite another thing, because the powers or
forces by which the machine continues to move are altogether independent of the artificer.

15. The phrase *intelligentia supramundana* may well be allowed, as it is
here explained, but without this explication, the expression is very apt to
lead to a wrong notion, as if God was not really and substantially present
everywhere.

16. To the questions proposed here the answer is: that God does always
act in the most regular and perfect manner, that there are no disorders in
the workmanship of God, and that there is nothing more extraordinary in
the alterations he is pleased to make in the frame of things than in his
continuation of it; that in things absolutely equal and indifferent in their
own nature, the will of God can freely choose and determine itself, without any external cause to impel it, and that it is a perfection in God to be
able so to do; that space does not at all depend on the order or situation or
existence of bodies.

17. And as to the notion of miracles, the question is not what it is that
theologians or philosophers usually allow or do not allow, but what reasons men advance for their opinions. If a miracle is only that which surpasses the power of all created beings, then for a man to walk on the water,
or for the motion of the sun or the earth to be stopped, is no miracle, since
none of these things require infinite power to effect them. For a body to
move in a circle around a center *in vacuo* if it is usual (as the planets moving about the sun), it is no miracle, whether it is effected immediately by
God himself or mediately by any created power; but if it is unusual (as for
a heavy body to be suspended and move so in the air), it is equally a miracle, whether it is effected immediately by God himself or mediately by any

50. Clarke notes that "The word *active force* signifies here nothing but motion
and the impetus or relative impulsive force of bodies arising from and being proportional to their motion. For, the occasion of what has passed upon this head was
the following passage." He then quotes from Newton's *Optics,* Query 31: "it appears that motion may be gotten or lost. But by reason of the tenacity of fluids and
attrition of their parts and the weakness of elasticity in solids, motion is much more
apt to be lost than gotten, and is always upon the decay. . . . Seeing therefore the
variety of motion which we find in the world is always decreasing, there is a necessity of conserving and recruiting it by active principles." See Appendix B, no. 3.

invisible created power. Lastly, if whatever does not arise from, and is not explicable by the natural powers of body is a miracle, then every animal motion whatsoever is a miracle. This seems demonstrably to show that this learned author's notion of a miracle is erroneous.

Leibniz's Fourth Letter, Being an Answer to Clarke's Third Reply[51]

1. In absolutely indifferent things there is [no foundation for] choice,[52] and consequently no election or will, since choice must be founded on some reason or principle.

2. A simple will without any motive[53] is a fiction, not only contrary to God's perfection, but also chimerical and contradictory, inconsistent with the definition of the will, and sufficiently refuted in my *Theodicy*.

3. It is an indifferent thing to place three bodies, equal and perfectly alike, in any order whatsoever, and consequently they will never be placed in any order by him who does nothing without wisdom.[54] But then, he being the author of things, no such things will be produced by him at all, and consequently there are no such things in nature.

4. There is no such thing as two individuals indiscernible from each other. An ingenious gentleman of my acquaintance, discoursing with me in the presence of Her Electoral Highness, the Princess Sophia, in the garden of Herrenhausen,[55] thought he could find two leaves perfectly alike. The princess defied him to do it, and he ran all over the garden a long time to look for some; but it was to no purpose. Two drops of water or milk, viewed with a microscope, will appear distinguishable from each other. This is an argument against atoms, which are confuted, as well as a vacuum, by the principles of true metaphysics.

5. Those great principles of *sufficient reason* and of the *identity of indiscernibles* change the state of metaphysics. That science becomes real and demonstrative by means of these principles, whereas before it did generally consist in empty words.

6. To suppose two things indiscernible is to suppose the same thing under two names. And therefore to suppose that the universe could have

51. June 2, 1716.

52. The bracketed remark is Clarke's addition; Leibniz had said "there is no choice at all."

53. Leibniz adds parenthetically "a mere will," aping Clarke's English.

54. See Appendix A, nos. 4 and 9.

55. Princess Sophia was Electress of Hanover and mother of George I of England; Herrenhausen was the residence of the Electors of Hanover.

had at first another position of time and place than that which it actually had, and yet that all the parts of the universe should have had the same situation among themselves as that which they actually had, such a supposition, I say, is an impossible fiction.

7. The same reason which shows that extramundane space is imaginary proves that all empty space is an imaginary thing, for they differ only as greater and less.

8. If space is a property or attribute, it must be the property of some substance. But what substance will that bounded empty space be an affection or property of, which the persons I am arguing with suppose to be between two bodies?

9. If infinite space is immensity, finite space will be the opposite to immensity, that is, it will be mensurability, or limited extension. Now extension must be the affection of something extended. But if that space is empty, it will be an attribute without a subject, an extension without anything extended. Thus, by making space a property, the author falls in with my opinion, which makes it an order of things and not anything absolute.

10. If space is an absolute reality, far from being a property or an accident opposed to substance, it will have a greater reality than substances themselves. God cannot destroy it, nor even change it in any respect. It will be not only immense in the whole but also immutable and eternal in every part. There will be an infinite number of eternal things besides God.

11. To say that infinite space has no parts is to say that it does not consist of finite spaces and that infinite space might subsist though all finite space should be reduced to nothing. It would be as if one should say, in accordance with the Cartesian supposition of a material extended unlimited world, that such a world might subsist, though all the bodies of which it consists should be reduced to nothing.

12. The author attributes parts to space, on p. 19 of the third edition of his *Defense of the Argument against Mr. Dodwell*,[56] and makes them inseparable one from another. But, on p. 30 of his *Second Defense,* he says they are parts "improperly so called," which may be understood in a good sense.

13. To say that God can cause the whole universe to move forward in a right line or in any other line, without making otherwise any alteration in it, is another chimerical supposition.[57] For two states indiscernible from each other are the same state, and consequently, it is a change without any change. Besides, there is neither rhyme nor reason in it. But God does

56. Clarke, *Works*, vol. III, pp. 763 and 794.
57. See Appendix A, no. 10.

nothing without reason, and it is impossible that there should be any here. Besides, it would be *agendo nihil agere*,[58] as I have just now said, because of the indiscernibility.

14. These are *idola tribus*[59] mere chimeras, and superficial imaginations. All this is only grounded on the supposition that imaginary space is real.

15. It is a like fiction, (that is) an impossible one, to suppose that God might have created the world some millions of years sooner. They who run into such kind of fictions can give no answer to those who would argue for the eternity of the world. For since God does nothing without reason, and no reason can be given why he did not create the world sooner, it will follow either that he has created nothing at all, or that he created the world before any assignable time, that is, that the world is eternal. But when once it has been shown that the beginning, whenever it was, is always the same thing, the question why it was not otherwise ordered becomes needless and insignificant.

16. If space and time were anything absolute, that is, if they were anything else besides certain orders of things, then indeed my assertion would be a contradiction. But since it is not so, the hypothesis [that space and time are anything absolute][60] is contradictory, that is, it is an impossible fiction.

17. And the case is the same as in geometry, where by the very supposition that a figure is greater than it really is, we sometimes prove that it is not greater. This indeed is a contradiction, but it lies in the hypothesis, which appears to be false for that very reason.

18. Space being uniform, there can be neither any external nor internal reason by which to distinguish its parts and to make any choice among them. For any external reason to discern between them can only be grounded on some internal one. Otherwise we should discern what is indiscernible or choose without discerning. A will without reason would be the chance of the Epicureans. A God who should act by such a will would be a God only in name. The cause of these errors proceeds from lack of care to avoid what derogates from the divine perfections.

19. When two incompatible things are equally good, and neither one of them has any advantage over the other, in themselves or by their combination with other things, God will produce neither of them.[61]

58. "In acting nothing would be done," that is, a change without any change.

59. "Idols of the tribe." See Bacon, *New Organon* I, aphorism 41.

60. Clarke's addition.

61. See Appendix A, nos. 4 and 9.

20. God is never determined by external things but always by what is in himself, that is, by his knowledge of things before anything exists outside himself.

21. There is no possible reason that can limit the quantity of matter, and therefore such limitation can have no place.

22. And supposing this arbitrary limitation of the quantity of matter, something might always be added to it without derogating from the perfection of those things which do already exist, and consequently something must always be added in order to act according to the principle of the perfection of the divine operations.

23. And therefore it cannot be said that the present quantity of matter is the fittest for the present constitution of things. And supposing it was, it would follow that this present constitution of things would not be the fittest absolutely, if it hinders God from using more matter. It is therefore better to choose another constitution of things, capable of something more.

24. I should be glad to see a passage of any philosopher who takes *sensorium* in any other sense than Goclenius does. [I was right in quoting the *Philosophical Dictionary* of this author to show the usual sense in which the word *sensorium* is taken; this is what dictionaries are for.][62]

25. If Scapula says that *sensorium* is the place in which the understanding resides, he means by it the organ of internal sensation. And therefore he does not differ from Goclenius.

26. *Sensorium* has always signified the organ of sensation. The pineal gland would be, according to Descartes, the *sensorium* in the above mentioned sense of Scapula.

27. There is hardly any less appropriate expression on this subject than that which gives God a sensorium. It seems to make God the soul of the world. And it will be a hard matter to put a justifiable sense on this word, according to the use Sir Isaac Newton makes of it.

28. Though the question is about the sense put on that word by Sir Isaac Newton, and not by Goclenius, yet I am not to blame for quoting the *Philosophical Dictionary* of that author, because the design of dictionaries is to show the use of words.

29. God consciously perceives things in himself. Space is the place of things and not the place of God's ideas, unless we look upon space as something that makes a union between God and things in imitation of the imagined union between the soul and the body, which would still make God the soul of the world.

---

62. The bracketed sentence was omitted by Clarke (perhaps because of its repetition in sec. 28).

30. And indeed, the author is much in the wrong when he compares God's knowledge and operation with the knowledge and operation of souls. The soul knows things because God has put into it a principle representative of outside things.[63] But God knows things because he produces them continually.

31. The soul does not act on things, according to my opinion, in any way other than because the body adapts itself to the desires of the soul, by virtue of the harmony which God has pre-established between them.[64]

32. But they who fancy that the soul can give a new force to the body, and that God does the same in the world in order to mend the imperfections of his machine, make God too much like the soul by ascribing too much to the soul and too little to God.

33. For none but God can give a new force to nature, and he does it only supernaturally. If there was need for him to do it in the natural course of things, he would have made a very imperfect work. At that rate, he would be with respect to the world what the soul, in the vulgar notion, is with respect to the body.

34. Those who undertake to defend the vulgar opinion concerning the soul's influence over the body by instancing God's operating on external things, make God still too much like a soul of the world. To which I add that the author's affecting to find fault with the words *intelligentia supramundana* seems also to incline that way.

35. The images with which the soul is immediately affected are within itself, but they correspond to those of the body. The presence of the soul is imperfect and can only be explained by that correspondence. But the presence of God is perfect and manifested by his operation.

36. The author wrongly supposes against me that the presence of the soul is connected with its influence over the body, for he knows I reject that influence.

37. The soul's being diffused through the brain is no less inexplicable than its being diffused through the whole body. The difference is only in more and less.

38. They who fancy that active forces decrease of themselves in the world do not well understand the principal laws of nature and the beauty of the works of God.[65]

39. How will they be able to prove that this defect is a consequence of the dependence of things?

63. See Appendix A, no. 11.
64. See Appendix A, no. 5.
65. Clarke refers to the footnote in sec. 13 of his *Third Reply*.

40. The imperfection of our machines, which is the reason why they need to be mended, proceeds from this very thing, that they do not sufficiently depend upon the workman. And therefore the dependence of nature on God, far from being the cause of such an imperfection, is rather the reason why there is no such imperfection in nature, because nature is so dependent on an artist who is too perfect to make a work that needs to be mended. It is true that every particular machine of nature is in some measure liable to be disordered, but not the whole universe, which cannot diminish in perfection.

41. The author contends that space does not depend on the situation of bodies. I answer: It is true, it does not depend on such or such a situation of bodies, but it is that order which renders bodies capable of being situated, and by which they have a situation among themselves when they exist together, as time is that order with respect to their successive position. But if there were no creatures, space and time would be only in the ideas of God.

42. The author seems to acknowledge here that his notion of a miracle is not the same as that which theologians and philosophers usually have. It is therefore sufficient for my purpose that my adversaries are obliged to have recourse to what is commonly called a miracle (which one attempts to avoid in philosophy).

43. I am afraid the author, by altering the sense commonly put on the word *miracle*, will fall into an inconvenient opinion. The nature of a miracle does not at all consist in usualness or unusualness, for then monsters would be miracles.

44. There are miracles of an inferior sort which an angel can work. He can, for instance, make a man walk upon the water without sinking. But there are miracles which none but God can work, they exceeding all natural powers. Of this kind are creating and annihilating.

45. It is also a supernatural thing that bodies should attract one another at a distance without any intermediate means and that a body should move around without receding in the tangent, though nothing hinders it from so receding. For these effects cannot be explained by the nature of things.

46. Why should it be impossible to explain the motion of animals by natural forces? Though, indeed, the beginning of animals is no less inexplicable by natural forces than the beginning of the world.

P.S.[66] All those who maintain a vacuum are more influenced by imagination than by reason. When I was a young man, I also gave in to the

---

66. This postscript was written by Leibniz as an addendum to a letter to Caroline dated May 12, 1716.

notion of a vacuum and atoms, but reason brought me into the right way. It was a pleasing imagination. Men carry their inquiries no further than those two things: they (as it were) nail down their thoughts to them; they fancy they have found out the first elements of things, a *non plus ultra*. We would have nature go no further, and be finite as our minds are; but this is being ignorant of the greatness and majesty of the author of things. The least corpuscle is actually subdivided to infinity and contains a world of other creatures that would be lacking in the universe, if that corpuscle was an atom, that is, a body of one entire piece without subdivision. In like manner, to admit a vacuum in nature is ascribing to God a very imperfect work; it is violating the great principle of the necessity of a sufficient reason, which many have talked of without understanding its true force; as I have lately shown in proving, by that principle, that space is only an order of things, as time also is, and not at all an absolute being. To omit many other arguments against a vacuum and atoms, I shall here mention those which I ground on God's perfection and on the necessity of a sufficient reason. I lay it down as a principle that every perfection which God could impart to things,[67] without derogating from their other perfections, has actually been imparted to them. Now let us fancy a wholly empty space. God could have placed some matter in it without derogating in any respect from all other things; therefore he has actually placed some matter in that space; therefore, there is no space wholly empty; therefore all is full. The same argument proves that there is no corpuscle but what is subdivided. I shall add another argument grounded on the necessity of a sufficient reason. It is impossible that there should be any principle to determine what proportion of matter there ought to be, out of all the possible degrees from a plenum to a vacuum, or from a vacuum to a plenum. Perhaps it will be said that the one should be equal to the other, but, because matter is more perfect than a vacuum, reason requires that a geometrical proportion should be observed and that there should be as much more matter than vacuum,[68] as the former deserves to be preferred. But then, there must be no vacuum at all, for the perfection of matter is to that of a vacuum as something to nothing. And the case is the same with atoms: what reason can anyone assign for confining nature in the progression of subdivision? These are fictions, merely arbitrary and unworthy of true philosophy. The reasons advanced for a vacuum are mere sophisms.

67. Clarke refers to sec. 9 of his *Third Reply* and to sec. 22 of his *Fourth Reply*.

68. Clarke refers again to sec. 9 of his *Third Reply* and to sec. 22 of his *Fourth Reply*.

Clarke's Fourth Reply[69]

1 and 2. This notion leads to universal necessity and fate, by supposing that motives have the same relation to the will of an intelligent agent as weights have to a balance,[70] so that, of two things absolutely indifferent, an intelligent agent can no more choose either than a balance can move itself when the weights on both sides are equal.[71] But the difference lies here. A balance is no agent but is merely passive and acted on by the weights, so that, when the weights are equal, there is nothing to move it. But intelligent beings are agents—not passive, in being moved by motives as a balance is by weights—but they have active powers and do move themselves, sometimes on the view of strong motives, sometimes on weak ones, and sometimes where things are absolutely indifferent. In this latter case, there may be very good reason to act, though two or more ways of acting may be absolutely indifferent. This learned writer always supposes the contrary as a principle, but gives no proof of it, either from the nature of things or the perfections of God.

3 and 4. This argument, if it was true, would prove that God neither has created nor can possibly create any matter at all.[72] For the perfectly solid parts of all matter, if you take them of equal figure and dimensions (which is always possible in supposition), are exactly alike, and therefore it would be perfectly indifferent if they were transposed in place; and consequently it was impossible (according to this learned author's argument) for God to place them in those places in which he did actually place them at the creation, because he might as easily have transposed their situation. It is very true that no two leaves, and perhaps no two drops of water, are exactly alike, because they are very much compounded bodies. But the case is very different in the parts of simple solid matter. And even in compounds, there is no impossibility for God to make two drops of water exactly alike. And if he should make them exactly alike, yet they would never the more become one and the same drop of water because they were alike. Nor would the place of the one be the place of the other, though it was absolutely indifferent which was placed in which place. The same reasoning holds likewise concerning the original determination of motion, this way or the contrary way.

5 and 6. Two things by being exactly alike do not cease to be two. The parts of time are as exactly alike to each other as those of space, yet two

69. June 26, 1716.

70. Clarke refers to sec. 1 of Leibniz's *Second Letter*. See also Appendix A, no. 3.

71. See Appendix A, no. 4.

72. See Appendix A, nos. 9 and 4.

points of time are not the same point of time, nor are they two names of only the same point of time. Had God created the world only at this moment, it would not have been created at the time it was created. And if God has made (or can make) matter finite in dimensions, the material universe must consequently be in its nature movable, for nothing that is finite is immovable. To say therefore that God could not have altered the time or place of the existence of matter is making matter necessarily infinite and eternal and reducing all things to necessity and fate.

7. Extramundane space (if the material world is finite in its dimensions) is not imaginary but real. Nor are void spaces in the world merely imaginary. In an exhausted receiver,[73] though rays of light, and perhaps some other matter, are there in an exceeding small quantity, still the lack of resistance plainly shows that the greatest part of that space is void of matter. For subtleness or fineness of matter cannot be the cause of lack of resistance. Quicksilver is as subtle and consists of as fine parts and as fluid as water, and yet makes more than ten times the resistance; this resistance arises therefore from the quantity and not from the grossness of the matter.

8. Space void of body is the property of an incorporeal substance. Space is not bounded by bodies but exists equally inside and outside bodies. Space is not enclosed between bodies, but bodies existing in unbounded space are themselves only terminated by their own dimensions.

9. Void space is not an attribute without a subject, because by void space we never mean space void of everything, but void of body only. In all void space God is certainly present, and possibly so are many other substances which are not matter, being neither tangible nor objects of any of our senses.

10. Space is not a substance but a property, and if it is a property of that which is necessary, it will consequently (as all other properties of that which is necessary must do) exist more necessarily (though it is not itself a substance) than those substances themselves which are not necessary. Space is immense and immutable and eternal, and so also is duration. Yet it does not at all follow from this that anything is eternal *hors de Dieu*.[74] For space and duration are not *hors de Dieu*, but are caused by and are immediate and necessary consequences of his existence.[75] And

---

73. Clarke indicates that the response was occasioned by a passage in the private letter (June 2, 1716; G VII, 378–9) with which Leibniz's *Fourth Letter* was enclosed.

74. "Outside of God."

75. Clarke quotes here from the General Scholium of the *Principia*: "He is eternal and infinite . . . cannot be never and nowhere. . . . God is omnipresent not only virtually but also substantially, for virtue cannot subsist without substances." See Appendix B, no. 2.

without them his eternity and ubiquity (or omnipresence) would be taken away.

11 and 12. Infinites are composed of finites in no other sense than as finites are composed of infinitesimals. In what sense space has or does not have parts has been explained before (*Third Reply*, sec. 3). Parts in the corporeal sense of the word are separable, compounded, ununited, independent of, and movable from each other; but infinite space, though it may be partially apprehended by us, that is, may in our imagination be conceived as composed of parts, yet since those parts (improperly so called) are essentially indiscernible and immovable from each other and not able to be parted without an express contradiction in terms (see above, *Second Reply*, sec. 4 and *Third Reply*, sec. 3), space consequently is in itself essentially one and absolutely indivisible.

13. If the world is finite in dimensions, it is movable by the power of God and therefore my argument drawn from that movableness is conclusive. Two places, though exactly alike, are not the same place. Nor is the motion or rest of the universe the same state,[76] any more than the motion or rest of a ship is the same state, because a man shut up in the cabin cannot perceive whether the ship sails or not, as long as it moves uniformly. The motion of the ship, though the man does not perceive it, is a real different state and has real different effects, and, on a sudden stop, it would have other real effects—and so likewise would an indiscernible motion of the universe. To this argument no answer has ever been given. It is largely insisted on by Sir Isaac Newton in his *Mathematical Principles* (definition 8) where, from the consideration of the properties, causes, and effects of motion, he shows the difference between real motion, or a body's being carried from one part of space to another, and relative motion, which is merely a change of the order or situation of bodies with respect to each other. This argument is a mathematical one, showing from real effects that there may be real motion where there is none relative, and relative motion where there is none real; it is not to be answered by barely asserting the contrary.

14. The reality of space is not a supposition, but is proved by the foregoing arguments to which no answer has been given. Nor is any answer given to that other argument, that space and time are quantities, which situation and order are not.

15. It was no impossibility for God to make the world sooner or later than he did, nor is it at all impossible for him to destroy it sooner or later than it shall actually be destroyed. As to the notion of the world's eternity, they who suppose matter and space to be the same must indeed

76. See Appendix A, no. 10.

suppose the world to be not only infinite and eternal, but necessarily so, even as necessarily as space and duration, which do not depend on the will but on the existence of God.[77] But they who believe that God created matter in what quantity, and at what particular time, and in what particular spaces he pleased are here under no difficulty. For the wisdom of God may have very good reasons for creating this world at that particular time he did, and may have made other kinds of things before this material world began, and may make other kinds of things after this world is destroyed.

16 and 17. That space and time are not the mere order of things but real quantities (which order and situation are not) has been proved above (See *Third Reply*, sec. 4, and in this paper, sec. 13), and no answer yet given to those proofs. And until an answer is given to those proofs, this learned author's assertion is (by his own confession in this place) a contradiction.

18. The uniformity of all the parts of space is no argument against God's acting in any part, after what manner he pleases. God may have good reasons to create finite beings, and finite beings can only be in particular places. And, all places being originally alike (even though place is nothing else but the situation of bodies), God's placing one cube of matter behind another equal cube of matter, rather than the other behind that, is a choice no way unworthy of the perfections of God, though both these situations are perfectly equal, because there may be very good reasons why both the cubes should exist, and they cannot exist but in one or other of equally reasonable situations. The Epicurean chance is not a choice of will but a blind necessity of fate.

19. This argument (as I now observed, sec. 3), if it proves anything, proves that God neither did nor can create any matter at all,[78] because the situation of equal and similar parts of matter could not but be originally indifferent, as was also the original determination of their motions this way or the contrary way.

20. I do not understand what this tends to prove with regard to the argument before us.

21. That God cannot limit the quantity of matter is an assertion of too great consequence to be admitted without proof. If he cannot limit the duration of it neither, then the material world is both infinite and eternal necessarily and independently of God.

22 and 23. This argument, if it is good, would prove that whatever God can do he cannot but do, and consequently that he cannot but make every-

---

77. See above, the footnote to sec. 10.
78. See Appendix A, nos. 9 and 4.

thing infinite and everything eternal. This is making him no governor at
all but a mere necessary agent, that is, indeed, no agent at all but mere fate
and nature and necessity.

24–28. Concerning the use of the word *sensory* (though Sir Isaac Newton says only "as it were the sensory"), enough has been said in my *Third
Reply*, sec. 10, *Second Reply*, sec. 3, and *First Reply*, sec. 3.

29. Space is the place of all things and of all ideas, just as duration is
the duration of all things and of all ideas. That this has no tendency to
make God the soul of the world, see above, *Second Reply*, sec. 12. There is
no union between God and the world. The mind of man might with
greater propriety be called the soul of the images of things it perceives
than God can be called the soul of the world, to which he is present
throughout and acts on it as he pleases, without being acted on by it.
Though this answer was given before (*Second Reply*, sec. 12), yet the
same objection is repeated again and again, without taking any notice of
the answer.

30. I do not understand what is meant by *representative principle*.[79] The
soul discerns things by having the images of things conveyed to it through
the organs of sense; God discerns things by being present to and in the
substances of the things themselves—not by producing them continually
(for he rests now from his work of creation), but by being continually
omnipresent to everything he created at the beginning.

31. That the soul should not operate on the body,[80] and yet the body by
mere mechanical impulse of matter conform itself to the will of the soul in
all the infinite variety of spontaneous animal motion, is a perpetual miracle. *Pre-established harmony* is a mere word or term of art and does nothing toward explaining the cause of so miraculous an effect.

32. To suppose that in spontaneous animal motion the soul gives no
new motion or impression to matter, but that all spontaneous animal
motion is performed by mechanical impulse of matter, is reducing all
things to mere fate and necessity. God's acting in the world on everything
after what manner he pleases, without any union and without being acted
on by anything, shows plainly the difference between an omnipresent governor and an imaginary soul of the world.

33. Every action is (in the nature of things) the giving of a new force to
the thing acted on. Otherwise it is not really action but mere passiveness,
as in the case of all mechanical and inanimate communications of motion.
If therefore the giving a new force is supernatural, then every action of
God is supernatural and he is quite excluded from the government of the

79. See Appendix A, no. 11.
80. See Appendix A, no. 3.

natural world, and every action of man is either supernatural, or else man is as mere a machine as a clock.

34 and 35. The difference between the true notion of God and that of a soul of the world has been before shown: *Second Reply* sec. 12 and in this paper, sec. 29 and 32.

36. This has been answered just above, sec. 31.

37. The soul is not diffused through the brain but is present to that particular place, which is the sensorium.

38. This is a bare assertion without proof. Two bodies void of elasticity meeting each other with equal contrary forces both lose their motion. And Sir Isaac Newton has given a mathematical instance (p. 341 of the Latin Edition of his *Optics*)[81] in which motion is continually diminishing and increasing in quantity, without any communication of this to other bodies.

39. This is no defect as is here supposed, but it is the just and proper nature of inert matter.

40. This argument (if it is good) proves that the material world must be infinite and that it must have been from eternity and must continue to eternity, and that God must always have created as many men and as many of all other things as it was possible for him to create and for as long a time also as it was possible for him to do it.

41. I do not understand what the meaning of these words is: "an order (or situation) which makes bodies capable of being situated." It seems to me to amount to this: that situation is the cause of situation. That space is not merely the order of bodies has been shown before (*Third Reply*, sec. 2 and 4), and that no answer has been given to the arguments there offered has been shown in this paper, sec. 13 and 14. Also that time is not merely the order of things succeeding each other is evident, because the quantity of time may be greater or less and yet that order continue the same. The order of things succeeding each other in time is not time itself, for they may succeed each other faster or slower in the same order of succession but not in the same time. If no creatures existed, still the ubiquity of God and the continuance of his existence would make space and duration to be exactly the same as they are now.[82]

42. This is appealing from reason to vulgar opinion, which philosophers should not do, because it is not the rule of truth.

43. Unusualness is necessarily included in the notion of a miracle. For otherwise there is nothing more wonderful, nor that requires greater power to effect, than some of those things we call natural, such as the

81. Query 31; see Appendix B, no. 3.
82. See above, the footnote to sec. 10.

motions of the heavenly bodies, the generation and formation of plants and animals, etc. Yet these are for this only reason not miracles, because they are common. Nevertheless, it does not follow that everything which is unusual is therefore a miracle. For it may be only the irregular and more rare effect of usual causes, of which kind are eclipses, monstrous births, madness in men, and innumerable things which the vulgar call prodigies.

[margin, handwritten: not every thing unusual is a miracle]

44. This is a concession of what I advanced. And yet it is contrary to the common opinion of theologians to suppose that an angel can work a miracle.

45. That one body should attract another without any intermediate means is indeed not a miracle but a contradiction, for it is supposing something to act where it is not. But the means by which two bodies attract each other may be invisible and intangible, and of a different nature from mechanism, and yet, acting regularly and constantly, may well be called natural, being much less wonderful than animal motion, which yet is never called a miracle.

46. If the word *natural forces* means here mechanical, then all animals, and even men, are as mere machines as a clock. But if the word does not mean mechanical forces, then gravitation may be effected by regular and natural powers, though they are not mechanical.

N.B. The arguments advanced in the postscript to Mr. Leibniz's fourth paper have been already answered in the foregoing replies. All that needs here to be observed is that his notion concerning the impossibility of physical atoms (for the question is not about mathematical atoms) is a manifest absurdity. For either there are or there are not any perfectly solid particles of matter. If there are any such, then the parts of such perfectly solid particles, taken of equal figure and dimensions (which is always possible in supposition), are perfectly alike physical atoms. But if there are no such perfectly solid particles, then there is no matter at all in the universe. For the further the division and subdivision of the parts of any body is carried before you arrive at parts perfectly solid and without pores, the greater is the proportion of pores to solid matter in that body. If therefore carrying on the division *in infinitum* you never arrive at parts perfectly solid and without pores, it will follow that all bodies consist of pores only, without any matter at all—which is a manifest absurdity. And the argument is the same with regard to the matter of which any particular species of bodies is composed, whether its pores are supposed empty or always full of extraneous matters.[83]

83. This sentence is added in the Errata.

Leibniz's Fifth Letter, Being an Answer to Clarke's Fourth Reply[84]

To Sections 1 and 2 of the Preceding Paper

1. I shall at this time reply more amply to clear the difficulties and to test whether the author is willing to listen to reason and to show that he is a lover of truth, or whether he will only quibble without clearing anything.

2. He often endeavors to impute to me necessity and fatality, though perhaps no one has better and more fully explained than I have done in my *Theodicy* the true difference between liberty, contingency, spontaneity, on the one side, and absolute necessity, chance, coaction, on the other. I do not know yet whether the author does this because he will do it, whatever I may say, or whether he does it (supposing him sincere in those imputations) because he has not yet duly considered my opinions. I shall soon find what I am to think of it, and I shall take my measures accordingly.

3. It is true that reasons in the mind of a wise being, and motives in any mind whatsoever, do that which answers to the effect produced by weights in a balance.[85] The author objects that this notion leads to necessity and fatality. But he says so without proving it and without taking notice of the explications I have formerly given in order to remove the difficulties that may be raised about that matter.

4. He also seems to play with equivocal terms. There are necessities that ought to be admitted. For we must distinguish between absolute and hypothetical necessity. We must also distinguish between a necessity that takes place because the opposite implies a contradiction (which necessity is called logical, metaphysical, or mathematical) and a necessity which is moral, by which a wise being chooses the best and every mind follows the strongest inclination.

5. Hypothetical necessity is that which the supposition or hypothesis of God's foresight and preordination imposes upon future contingents. And this must necessarily be admitted, unless we deny, as the Socinians do, God's foreknowledge of future contingents and his providence which regulates and governs every particular thing.

---

84. August 18, 1716. Leibniz made many additions and corrections in the margins of the copy of the letter he sent to Pierre Des Maizeaux. Clarke took account of these changes in his published version of Leibniz's *Fifth Letter* in French. The following note occurs at the beginning of that letter: "The variant readings printed in the margin of the following paper are changes made in Leibniz's own hand in another copy of this paper which he sent to one of his friends in England a short time before his death." We have inserted the changes within angle brackets in the text.

85. See Appendix A, no. 3.

6. But neither that foreknowledge nor that preordination derogate from liberty. For God, being moved by his supreme reason to choose, among many series of things or possible worlds, that in which free creatures should take such or such resolutions, though not without his concourse, has thereby rendered every event certain and determined once for all, without thereby derogating from the liberty of those creatures that simple decree of choice, not at all changing but only actualizing their free natures which he saw in his ideas.

7. As for moral necessity, this also does not derogate from liberty. For when a wise being, and especially God who has supreme wisdom, chooses what is best, he is not the less free on that account; on the contrary, it is the most perfect liberty not to be hindered from acting in the best manner. And when any other chooses according to the most apparent and the most strongly inclining good, he imitates in this the liberty of a truly wise being, in proportion to his disposition. Without this, the choice would be a blind chance.

8. But good, either true or apparent—in a word, the motive—inclines without necessitating, that is, without imposing an absolute necessity. For when God (for instance) chooses the best, what he does not choose, and is inferior in perfection, is nevertheless possible. But if what he chooses was absolutely necessary, any other way would be impossible—which is against the hypothesis. For God chooses among possibles, that is, among many ways none of which implies a contradiction.

9. But to say that God can only choose what is best, and to infer from this that what he does not choose is impossible, this, I say, is confounding of terms; it is blending power and will, metaphysical necessity and moral necessity, essences and existences. For what is necessary is so by its essence, since the opposite implies a contradiction; but a contingent that exists owes its existence to the principle of what is best, which is a sufficient reason for the existence of things. And therefore I say that motives incline without necessitating, and that there is a certainty and infallibility, but not an absolute necessity in contingent things. Add to this what will be said below, in nos. 73 and 76.

10. And I have sufficiently shown in my *Theodicy* that this moral necessity is a good thing, agreeable to the divine perfection, agreeable to the great principle or ground of existences, which is that of the need for a sufficient reason, whereas absolute and metaphysical necessity depends on the other great principle of our reasonings, namely, that of essences, that is, the principle of identity or contradiction. For what is absolutely necessary is the only possible way, and its contrary implies a contradiction.

11. I have also shown that our will does not always exactly follow the

practical understanding, because it may have or find reasons to suspend its resolution until a further examination.

12. To impute to me after this the notion of an absolute necessity, without having anything to say against the reasons which I have just now advanced and which go to the bottom of things, perhaps beyond what is to be seen elsewhere, this, I say, will be an unreasonable obstinacy.

13. As to the notion of fatality which the author also lays to my charge, this is another ambiguity. There is a *fatum Mahometanum,* a *fatum Stoicum,* and a *fatum Christianum.* The Turkish fate will have an effect happen even though its cause should be avoided, as if there was an absolute necessity. The Stoical fate will have a man be quiet because he must have patience whether he will or not, since it is impossible to resist the course of things. But it is agreed that there is *fatum Christianum,* a certain destiny of everything, regulated by the foreknowledge and providence of God. *Fatum* is derived from *fari,* that is, *to pronounce, to decree,* and in its right sense it signifies the decree of providence. And those who submit to it through a knowledge of the divine perfections, of which the love of God is a consequence <since it consists in the pleasure which this knowledge gives>, have not only patience like the heathen philosophers, but are also contented with what is ordained by God, knowing he does everything for the best and not only for the greatest good in general, but also for the greatest particular good of those who love him.

14. I have been obliged to enlarge in order to remove ill-grounded imputations once for all, as I hope I shall be able to do by these explanations, so as to satisfy fair-minded persons. I shall now come to an objection raised here against my comparing the weights of a balance with the motives of the will. It is objected that a balance is merely passive and moved by the weights, whereas intelligent agents endowed with will are active. To this I answer that the principle of the need for a sufficient reason is common both to agents and patients;[86] they need a sufficient reason for their action as well as for their passion. A balance not only does not act when it is equally pulled on both sides, but the equal weights likewise do not act when they are in an equilibrium, so that one of them cannot go down without the others rising up as much.

15. It must also be considered that, properly speaking, motives do not act on the mind as weights do on a balance, but it is rather the mind that acts by virtue of the motives, which are its dispositions to act. And therefore to claim, as the author does here, that the mind sometimes prefers weak motives to strong ones, and even that it prefers that which is indifferent before motives, this, I say, is to divide the mind from the motives,

86. See Appendix A, no. 3.

as if they were outside the mind as the weight is distinct from the balance and as if the mind had, besides motives, other dispositions to act by virtue of which it could reject or accept the motives. Whereas, in truth, the motives comprehend all the dispositions which the mind can have to act voluntarily, for they include not only the reasons, but also the inclinations arising from passions or other preceding impressions. For this reason, if the mind should prefer a weak inclination to a strong one, it would act against itself and otherwise than it is disposed to act. This shows that the author's notions, contrary to mine, are superficial and appear to have no solidity in them when they are well considered.

16. To assert also that the mind may have good reasons to act when it has no motives and when things are absolutely indifferent, as the author explains himself here, this, I say, is a manifest contradiction. For if the mind has good reasons for taking the part it takes, then the things are not indifferent to the mind.

17. And to affirm that the mind will act when it has reasons to act, even though the ways of acting were absolutely indifferent, this, I say, is to speak again very superficially and in a manner that cannot be defended. For a man never has a sufficient reason to act when he does not also have a sufficient reason to act in a certain particular manner, every action being individual and not general, nor abstract from its circumstances, but always needing some particular way of being put in execution. For this reason, when there is a sufficient reason to do any particular thing, there is also a sufficient reason to do it in a certain particular manner; and consequently several manners of doing it are not indifferent. As often as a man has sufficient reasons for a single action, he has also sufficient reasons for all its requirements. See also what I shall say below, no. 66.

18. These arguments are very obvious, and it is very strange to charge me with advancing my principle of the need for a sufficient reason without any proof drawn either from the nature of things or from the divine perfections. For the nature of things requires that every event should have beforehand its proper conditions, requirements, and dispositions, the existence of which makes the sufficient reason of such an event.

19. And God's perfection requires that all his actions should be agreeable to his wisdom and that it may not be said of him that he has acted without reason, or even that he has preferred a weaker reason before a stronger.

20. But I shall speak more largely at the conclusion of this paper concerning the solidity and importance of this great principle of the need for a sufficient reason for every event, the overthrowing of which principle would overthrow the best part of all philosophy. It is therefore very strange that the author should say I am guilty of begging the question in

this, and it plainly appears he is desirous to maintain indefensible opinions, since he is reduced to deny that great principle which is one of the most essential principles of reason.

To Sections 3 and 4

21. It must be confessed that though this great principle has been acknowledged, yet it has not been sufficiently made use of. This is in great measure the reason why first philosophy[87] has not been as fruitful and demonstrative up to now as it should have been. I infer from that principle, among other consequences, that there are not in nature two real, absolute beings, indiscernible from each other, because if there were, God and nature would act without reason in treating the one otherwise than the other, and that therefore God does not produce two pieces of matter perfectly equal and alike. The author answers this conclusion without refuting its reason, and he answers with a very weak objection. "That argument," he says, "if it was good, would prove that it would be impossible for God to create any matter at all. For the perfectly solid parts of matter, if we take them of equal figure and dimensions (which is always possible in supposition), would be exactly alike." But it is manifestly begging the question to suppose that perfect likeness, which, according to me, cannot be admitted. This supposition of two indiscernibles, such as two pieces of matter perfectly alike, seems indeed to be possible in abstract terms, but it is not consistent with the order of things, nor with the divine wisdom by which nothing is admitted without reason. The vulgar fancy such things because they content themselves with incomplete notions. And this is one of the faults of the atomists.

22. Besides, I do not admit in matter parts perfectly solid, or that are the same throughout without any variety or particular motion in their parts, as the pretended atoms are imagined to be. To suppose such bodies is another ill-grounded popular opinion. According to my demonstrations, every part of matter is actually subdivided into parts differently moved, and no one of them is perfectly like another.

23. I said that in sensible things two that are indiscernible from each other can never be found, that (for instance) two leaves in a garden or two drops of water perfectly alike are not to be found. The author acknowledges it as to leaves and perhaps as to drops of water. But he might have admitted it without any hesitation, without a *perhaps* (an Italian would say *senza forse*), as to drops of water likewise.

24. I believe that these general observations in things sensible hold also

87. That is, metaphysics.

in proportion in things insensible, and that one may say in this respect what Harlequin says in the *Emperor of the Moon*: it is there, just as it is here. And it is a great objection against indiscernibles that no instance of them is to be found. But the author opposes this consequence, because (he says) sensible bodies are composed, whereas he maintains there are insensible bodies which are simple. I answer again that I do not admit simple bodies. There is nothing simple in my opinion but true monads, which have neither parts nor extension. Simple bodies, and even perfectly similar ones, are a consequence of the false hypothesis of a vacuum and of atoms, or of lazy philosophy, which does not sufficiently carry on the analysis of things and fancies it can attain to the first material elements of nature, because our imagination would be satisfied with this.

25. When I deny that there are two drops of water perfectly alike, or any two other bodies indiscernible from each other, I do not say it is absolutely impossible to suppose them, but that it is a thing contrary to the divine wisdom, and which consequently does not exist.

To Sections 5 and 6

26. I admit that if two things perfectly indiscernible from each other did exist, they would be two, but that supposition is false and contrary to the great principle of reason. The vulgar philosophers were mistaken when they believed that there are things different *solo numero*,[88] or only because they are two, and from this error have arisen their perplexities about what they called *the principle of individuation*. Metaphysics has generally been handled like a science of mere words, like a philosophical dictionary, without entering into the discussion of things. Superficial philosophy, such as is that of the atomists and vacuists, forges things which superior reasons do not admit. I hope my demonstrations will change the face of philosophy, notwithstanding such weak objections as the author raises here against me.

27. The parts of time or place considered in themselves are ideal things, and therefore they perfectly resemble one another like two abstract units. But it is not so with two concrete ones, or with two real times, or two spaces filled up, that is, truly actual.

28. I do not say that two points of space are one and the same point, nor that two instants of time are one and the same instant, as the author seems to charge me with saying. But a man may fancy, for lack of knowledge, that there are two different instants where there is but one; in like manner, as I observed in section seventeen of the preceding answer, that

88. "In number alone."

frequently in geometry we suppose two, in order to represent the error of a refuter, when there is really but one. If any man should suppose that a right line cuts another in two points, it will be found after all that those two pretended points must coincide and make but one point.

29. I have demonstrated that space is nothing else but an order of the existence of things observed as existing together, and therefore the fiction of a material finite universe moving forward in an infinite empty space cannot be admitted.[89] It is altogether unreasonable and impracticable. For besides the fact that there is no real space out of the material universe, such an action would be without any design in it; it would be working without doing anything, *agendo nihil agere*.[90] There would happen no change which could be observed by any person whatsoever. These are imaginations of philosophers who have incomplete notions, who make space an absolute reality. Mere mathematicians who are only taken up with the conceits of imagination are apt to forge such notions, but they are destroyed by superior reasons.

30. Absolutely speaking, it appears that God can make the material universe finite in extension, but the contrary appears more agreeable to his wisdom.

31. I do not grant that every finite is movable. According to the hypothesis of my adversaries themselves, a part of space, though finite, is not movable. What is movable must be capable of changing its situation with respect to something else and to be in a new state discernible from the first; otherwise the change is but a fiction. A movable finite must therefore make part of another finite, so that any change may happen which can be observed.

32. Descartes maintains that matter is unlimited, and I do not think he has been sufficiently confuted. And though this is granted him, it does not follow that matter would be necessary, nor that it would have existed from all eternity, since that unlimited diffusion of matter would only be an effect of God's choice judging that to be the better.

To Section 7

33. Since space in itself is an ideal thing like time, space out of the world must necessarily be imaginary, as the schoolmen themselves have acknowledged. The case is the same with empty space within the world, which I take also to be imaginary, for the reasons before adduced.

34. The author objects against me the vacuum discovered by Mr.

89. See Appendix A, no. 10.
90. "In acting nothing would be done."

Guericke[91] of Magdeburg, which is made by pumping the air out of a receiver, and he claims that there is truly a perfect vacuum or a space without matter (at least in part) in that receiver. The Aristotelians and Cartesians, who do not admit a true vacuum, have said in answer to that experiment of Mr. Guericke, as well as to that of Torricelli[92] of Florence (who emptied the air out of a glass tube by the help of mercury), that there is no vacuum at all in the tube or in the receiver, since glass has small pores which the beams of light, the effluvia of the magnet, and other very thin fluids may go through. I am of their opinion, and I think the receiver may be compared to a box full of holes in the water, having fish or other gross bodies shut up in it, which, being taken out, their place would nevertheless be filled up with water. There is only this difference: that though water is fluid and more yielding than those gross bodies, yet it is as heavy and massive, if not more, than they, whereas the matter which gets into the receiver in the room of the air is much more subtle. The new partisans of a vacuum advance in answer to this instance that it is not the grossness of matter but its mere quantity that makes resistance, and consequently that there is of necessity more vacuum where there is less resistance. They add that the subtleness of matter has nothing to do here and that the particles of quicksilver are as subtle and fine as those of water, and yet that quicksilver resists about ten times more. To this I reply that it is not so much the quantity of matter as its difficulty of giving place that makes resistance. For instance, floating timber contains less of heavy matter than an equal bulk of water does, and yet it makes more resistance to a boat than the water does.

35. And as for quicksilver, it is true that it contains about fourteen times more of heavy matter than an equal bulk of water does, but it does not follow that it contains fourteen times more matter absolutely. On the contrary, water contains as much matter, if we include both its own matter, which is heavy, and the extraneous matter void of heaviness which passes through its pores. For both quicksilver and water are masses of heavy matter, full of pores, through which there passes a great deal of matter void of heaviness <and which makes no sensible resistance>, such as is probably that of the rays of light and other insensible fluids, and especially that which is itself the cause of the gravity of gross bodies by receding from the center toward which it drives those bodies. For it is a strange imagination to make all matter gravitate, and that toward all other matter, as if each body did equally attract every other body according to

91. Otto von Guericke (1602–1686) was an experimentalist and the inventor of the air pump.

92. Evangelista Torricelli (1608–1647) was Galileo's student and the inventor of the barometer.

their masses and distances, and this by an attraction properly so called, which is not derived from an occult impulse of bodies, whereas the gravity of sensible bodies toward the center of the earth ought to be produced by the motion of some fluid. And the case must be the same with other gravities, such as is that of the planets toward the sun or toward each other. <A body is never moved naturally except by another body that touches it and pushes it; after that it continues until it is prevented by another body that touches it. Any other kind of operation on bodies is either miraculous or imaginary>.

To Sections 8 and 9

36. I objected that space, taken for something real and absolute without bodies, would be a thing eternal, unaffected, and independent of God. The author endeavors to elude this difficulty by saying that space is a property of God. In answer to this I have said, in my foregoing paper, that the property of God is immensity but that space (which is often commensurate with bodies) and God's immensity are not the same thing.

37. I objected further that if space is a property, and infinite space is the immensity of God, finite space will be the extension or measurability of something finite. And therefore the space taken up by a body will be the extension of that body. This is an absurdity, since a body can change space but cannot leave its extension.

38. I asked also, if space is a property, what thing will an empty limited space (such as that which my adversary imagines in an exhausted receiver) be the property of? It does not appear reasonable to say that this empty space, either round or square, is a property of God. Will it be then perhaps the property of some immaterial, extended, imaginary substances which the author seems to fancy in the imaginary spaces?

39. If space is the property or affection of the substance which is in space, the same space will be sometimes the affection of one body, sometimes of another body, sometimes of an immaterial substance, and sometimes perhaps of God himself, when it is void of all other substance, material or immaterial. But this is a strange property or affection, which passes from one subject to another. Thus subjects will leave off their accidents, like clothes, so that other subjects may put them on. At this rate how shall we distinguish accidents and substances?

40. And if limited spaces are the affections of limited substances which are in them, and infinite space is a property of God, a property of God must (which is very strange) be made up of the affections of creatures, for all finite spaces taken together make up infinite space.

41. But if the author denies that limited space is an affection of limited

things, it will not be reasonable either that infinite space should be the affection or property of an infinite thing. I have suggested all these difficulties in my foregoing paper, but it does not appear that the author has endeavored to answer them.

42. I have still other reasons against this strange imagination that space is a property of God. If it is so, space belongs to the essence of God. But space has parts; therefore there would be parts in the essence of God. *Spectatum admissi.*[93]

43. Moreover, spaces are sometimes empty and sometimes filled up. Therefore there will be in the essence of God parts sometimes empty and sometimes full and consequently liable to a perpetual change. Bodies filling up space would fill up part of God's essence and would be commensurate with it; and in the supposition of a vacuum, part of God's essence will be within the receiver. Such a God having parts will very much resemble the Stoics' God, which was the whole universe considered as a divine animal.

44. If infinite space is God's immensity, infinite time will be God's eternity; and therefore we must say that what is in space is in God's immensity, and consequently in his essence, and that what is in time <is in the eternity of God and> is also in the essence of God. Strange expressions, which plainly show that the author makes a wrong use of terms.

45. I shall give another instance of this. God's immensity makes him actually present in all spaces. But now if God is in space, how can it be said that space is in God or that it is a property of God? We have often heard that a property is in its subject, but we never heard that a subject is in its property. In like manner, God exists in all time. How then can time be in God, and how can it be a property of God? These are perpetual *alloglossies.*[94]

46. It appears that the author confounds immensity, or the extension of things, with the space according to which that extension is taken. Infinite space is not the immensity of God; finite space is not the extension of bodies, as time is not their duration. Things keep their extension, but they do not always keep their space. Everything has its own extension, its own duration, but it does not have its own time and does not keep its own space.

47. I will here show how men come to form the notion of space to themselves. They consider that many things exist at once, and they observe in them a certain order of coexistence, according to which the relation of one thing to another is more or less simple. This order is their

---

93. This is a reference to Horace, *De Arte Poetica*, 1.5: "Spectatum admissi risum teneatis amici [If you saw such a thing, could you refrain your laughter, friends]?"

94. That is, barbaric or strange expressions.

situation or distance. When it happens that one of those coexistent things changes its relation to a multitude of others which do not change their relation among themselves, and that another thing, newly come, acquires the same relation to the others as the former had, we then say that it is come into the place of the former; and this change we call a motion in that body in which is the immediate cause of the change. And though many, or even all, the coexistent things should change according to certain known rules of direction and speed, yet one may always determine the relation of situation which every coexistent acquires with respect to every other coexistent, and even that relation which any other coexistent would have to this, or which this would have to any other, if it had not changed or if it had changed any other way. And supposing or feigning that among those coexistents there is a sufficient number of them which have undergone no change, then we may say that those which have such a relation to those fixed existents as others had to them before, have now the *same place* which those others had. And that which comprehends all those places is called *space*. This shows that, in order to have an idea of place and consequently of space, it is sufficient to consider these relations and the rules of their changes, without needing to fancy any absolute reality out of the things whose situation we consider. And, to give a kind of a definition: *place* is that which we say is the same to A and to B when the relation of the coexistence of B with C, E, F, G, etc. agrees perfectly with the relation of the coexistence which A had with the same C, E, F, G, etc., supposing there has been no cause of change in C, E, F, G, etc. It may be said also, without entering into any further particularity, that *place* is that which is the same in different moments to different existent things when their relations of coexistence with certain other existents which are supposed to continue fixed from one of those moments to the other agree entirely together. And *fixed existents* are those in which there has been no cause of any change of the order of their coexistence with others, or (which is the same thing) in which there has been no motion. Lastly, *space* is that which results from places taken together. And here it may not be amiss to consider the difference between place and the relation of situation which is in the body that fills up the place. For the place of A and B is the same, whereas the relation of A to fixed bodies is not precisely and individually the same as the relation which B (that comes into its place) will have to the same fixed bodies; but these relations agree only. For two different subjects, such as A and B, cannot have precisely the same individual affection, since it is impossible that the same individual accident should be in two subjects or pass from one subject to another. But the mind, not contented with an agreement, looks for an identity, for something that should be truly the same, and conceives it as being extrinsic to the subjects; and this is what we call *place* and *space*. But this can only be an ideal thing, containing a certain order, in which the mind conceives the application of relations. In like manner, as the mind can fancy to itself an order made up of genealogical lines whose size would consist only in the number of generations, in which every person would have his place; and if should add to this one the fiction of a metempsychosis and bring in the same human souls again, the persons in those lines might change place; he who was a father or a grandfather might become a son or a grandson, etc. And yet those genealogical places, lines, and spaces, though they should express real truth, would only be ideal things. I shall adduce another example to show how the mind uses, on occasion of accidents which are in subjects, to fancy to itself something answerable to those accidents out of the subjects. The ratio or proportion between two lines L and M may be conceived three several ways: as a ratio of the greater L to the lesser M; as a ratio of the lesser M to the greater L; and lastly as something abstracted from both, that is, as the ratio between L and M without considering which is the antecedent or which the consequent, which the subject and which the object. And thus it is that proportions are considered in music. In the first way of considering them, L the greater, in the second, M the lesser, is the subject of that accident which philosophers call relation. But which of them will be the subject in the third way of considering them? It cannot be said that both of them, L and M together, are the subject of such an accident; for if so, we should have an accident in two subjects, with one leg in one and the other in the other, which is contrary to the notion of accidents. Therefore we must say that this relation, in this third way of considering it, is indeed out of the subjects; but being neither a substance nor an accident, it must be a mere ideal thing, the consideration of which is nevertheless useful. To conclude, I have done here much like Euclid, who, not being able to make his readers well understand what *ratio* is absolutely in the sense of geometers, defines what are the *same ratios*. Thus, in like manner, in order to explain what *place is*, I have been content to define what is the *same place*. Lastly, I observe that the traces of movable bodies, which they leave sometimes on the immovable ones on which they are moved, have given men occasion to form such an idea in their imagination, as if some trace did still remain even when there is nothing unmoved. But this is a mere ideal thing and imports only that if there was any unmoved thing there, the trace might be marked out on it. And it is this analogy which makes men fancy places, traces, and spaces, though those things consist only in the truth of relations, and not at all in any absolute reality.

48. To conclude, if the space (which the author fancies) void of all bodies is not altogether empty, what is it then full of? Is it full of extended

spirits perhaps, or immaterial substances capable of extending and contracting themselves, which move in there and penetrate each other without any inconvenience, as the shadows of two bodies penetrate one another on the surface of a wall? I think I see the revival of the odd imaginations of Dr. Henry More (otherwise a learned and well-meaning man) and of some others who fancied that those spirits can make themselves impenetrable whenever they please. No, some have fancied that man in the state of innocence also had the gift of penetration, and that he became solid, opaque, and impenetrable by his fall. Is it not overthrowing our notions of things to make God have parts, to make spirits have extension? The principle of the need for a sufficient reason does alone drive away all these specters of imagination. Men easily run into fictions for lack of making a right use of that great principle.

To Section 10

49. It cannot be said that <a certain> duration is eternal but <it can be said> that the things which continue always are eternal <always gaining a new duration>. Whatever exists of time and of duration <being successive>, perishes continually, and how can a thing exist eternally which (to speak exactly) never does exist at all? For how can a thing exist of which no part ever does exist? Nothing of time does ever exist but instants, and an instant is not even itself a part of time. Whoever considers these observations will easily apprehend that time can only be an ideal thing. And the analogy between time and space will easily make it appear that the one is as merely ideal as the other. <But if in saying that the duration of a thing is eternal, it is only meant that the thing endures eternally, I have nothing to say against it.>

50. If the reality of space and time is necessary to the immensity and eternity of God, if God must be in space, if being in space is a property of God, he will in some measure depend on time and space and stand in need of them. For I have already prevented that subterfuge—that space and time are <in God and like> properties of God. <Could one maintain the opinion that bodies move in the parts of the divine essence?>

To Sections 11 and 12

51. I objected that space cannot be in God because it has parts. Hereupon the author seeks another subterfuge by departing from the received sense of words, maintaining that space has no parts because its parts are not separable and cannot be removed from one another by being plucked out. But it is sufficient that space has parts, whether those parts are sepa-

rable or not, and they may be assigned in space, either by the bodies that are in it or by lines and surfaces that may be drawn and described in it.

To Section 13

52. In order to prove that space without bodies is an absolute reality, the author objected that a finite material universe might move forward in space. I answered that it does not appear reasonable that the material universe should be finite; and although we should suppose it to be finite, yet it is unreasonable it should have motion otherwise than as its parts change their situation among themselves, because such a motion would produce no change that could be observed[95] and would be without design. It is another thing when its parts change their situation among themselves, for then there is a motion in space, but it consists in the order of relations which are changed. The author replies now that the reality of motion does not depend on being observed, and that a ship may go forward, and yet a man who is in the ship may not consciously perceive it. I answer that motion does not indeed depend on being observed, but it does depend on being able to be observed. There is no motion when there is no change that can be observed. And when there is no change that can be observed, there is no change at all. The contrary opinion is grounded on the supposition of a real absolute space, which I have demonstratively refuted by the principle of the need for a sufficient reason of things.

53. I find nothing in the eighth definition of the *Mathematical Principles of Nature*, nor in the scholium belonging to it, that proves or can prove the reality of space in itself.[96] However, I grant there is a difference between an absolute true motion of a body and a mere relative change of its situation with respect to another body. For when the immediate cause of the change is in the body, that body is truly in motion, and then the situation of other bodies, with respect to it will be changed consequently, though the cause of that change is not in them. It is true that, exactly speaking, there is not any one body that is perfectly and entirely at rest, but we frame an abstract notion of rest by considering the thing mathematically. Thus have I left nothing unanswered of what has been advanced for the absolute reality of space. And I have demonstrated the falsehood of that reality by a fundamental principle, one of the most certain both in reason and experience, against which no exception or instance can be advanced. On the whole, one may judge from what has been said that I must not admit a movable universe, nor any place out of the material universe.

95. See Appendix A, no. 10.
96. See Appendix B, no. 1.

To Section 14

54. I am not aware of any objection but what I think I have sufficiently answered. As for the objection that space and time are quantities, or rather things endowed with quantity, and that situation and order are not so, I answer that order also has its quantity: there is in it that which goes before and that which follows; there is distance or interval. Relative things have their quantity as well as absolute ones. For instance, ratios or proportions in mathematics have their quantity and are measured by logarithms, and yet they are relations. And therefore though time and space consist in relations, still they have their quantity.

To Section 15

55. As to the question whether God could have created the world sooner, it is necessary here to understand each other rightly. Since I have demonstrated that time without things is nothing else but a mere ideal possibility, it is manifest that if anyone should say that this same world which has been actually created might have been created sooner without any other change, he would say nothing that is intelligible. For there is no mark or difference by which it would be possible to know that this world was created sooner. And therefore (as I have already said) to suppose that God created the same world sooner is supposing a chimerical thing. It is making time an absolute thing, independent of God, whereas time does only coexist with creatures and is only conceived by the order and quantity of their changes.

56. But yet absolutely speaking one may conceive that an universe began sooner than it actually did. Let us suppose our universe or any other to be represented by the Figure AF, and that the ordinate AB represents its first state and the ordinates CD and EF its following states; I say one may conceive that such a world began sooner by conceiving the figure prolonged backwards, and by adding to it SRABS. For thus, things being increased, time will be also increased. But whether such an augmentation is reasonable and agreeable to God's wisdom is another question to which we answer in the negative; otherwise God would have made such an augmentation. It

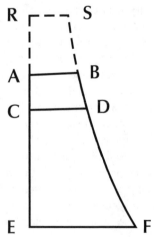

would be like as *Humano capiti cervicem pictor equinam jungere si velit.*[97] The case is the same with respect to the destruction[98] of the universe. As one might conceive something added to the beginning, so one might also conceive something taken off toward the end. But such a retrenching from it would be also unreasonable.

57. Thus it appears how we are to understand that God created things at what time he pleased, for this depends on the things he resolved to create. But things being once resolved on, together with their relations, there remains no longer any choice about the time and the place, which of themselves have nothing in them real, nothing that can distinguish them, nothing that is at all discernible.

58. One cannot therefore say, as the author does here, that the wisdom of God may have good reasons to create this world[99] at such or such a particular time, since that particular time considered without the things is an impossible fiction, and good reasons for a choice are not to be found where everything is indiscernible.

59. When I speak of this world, I mean the whole universe of material and immaterial creatures taken together, from the beginning of things. But if anyone means only the beginning of the material world, and supposes immaterial creatures before it, he would have somewhat more reason for his supposition. For time then being marked by things that existed already, it would be no longer indifferent, and there might be room for choice. And yet, indeed, this would be only putting off the difficulty. For supposing the whole universe of immaterial and material creatures together to have a beginning, there is no longer any choice about the time in which God would place that beginning.

60. And therefore one must not say, as the author does here, that God created things in what particular space and at what particular time he pleased. For all time and all spaces being in themselves perfectly uniform and indiscernible from each other, one of them cannot please more than another.

61. I shall not enlarge here on my opinion explained elsewhere that there are no created substances wholly destitute of matter. For I hold with the ancients and according to reason that angels or intelligences, and souls separated from a gross body, always have subtle bodies, though they

97. "If a painter wished to join the neck of a horse to a human head . . ." Horace, *De Arte Poetica.* The sentence ends with the verse quoted in no. 42: "If you saw such a thing, could you refrain your laughter, friends?"

98. G VII, 405 has *duration.*

99. *"Ce monde"*; Leibniz adds parenthetically "this world," emphasizing Clarke's English expression.

themselves are incorporeal. The vulgar philosophy easily admits all sorts of fictions; mine is more strict.

62. I do not say that matter and space are the same thing. I only say that there is no space where there is no matter and that space in itself is not an absolute reality. Space and matter differ as time and motion. However, these things, though different, are inseparable.

63. But yet it does not at all follow that matter is eternal and necessary, unless we suppose space to be eternal and necessary—a supposition ill grounded in all respects.

To Sections 16 and 17

64. I think I have answered everything, and I have particularly replied to that objection that space and time have quantity and that order has none. See above, no. 54.

65. I have clearly shown that the contradiction lies in the hypothesis of the opposite opinion, which looks for a difference where there is none. And it would be a manifest iniquity to infer from this that I have acknowledged a contradiction in my own opinion.

To Section 18

66. Here I find again an argument which I have overthrown above, no. 17. The author says that God may have good reasons to make two cubes perfectly equal and alike, and then (he says) God must necessarily assign them their places, although every other respect is perfectly equal. But things ought not to be separated from their circumstances. This argument consists in incomplete notions. God's resolutions are never abstract and imperfect, as if God decreed first to create the two cubes and then made another decree where to place them. Men, being such limited creatures as they are, may act in this manner. They may resolve on a thing and then find themselves perplexed about means, ways, places, and circumstances. But God never takes a resolution about the ends without resolving at the same time about the means and all the circumstances. No, I have shown in my *Theodicy* that, properly speaking, there is but one decree for the whole universe, by which God resolved to bring it out of possibility into existence. And therefore God will not choose a cube without choosing its place at the same time, and he will never choose among indiscernibles.

67. The parts of space are not determined and distinguished only by the things which are in it, and the diversity of things in space determines God to act differently on different parts of space. But space without

things has nothing by which it may be distinguished and, indeed, not anything actual.

68. If God is resolved to place a certain cube of matter at all, he is also resolved in what particular place to put it. But it is with respect to other parts of matter, and not with respect to bare space itself, in which there is nothing to distinguish it.

69. But wisdom does not allow God to place at the same time two cubes perfectly equal and alike, because there is no way to find any reason for assigning them different places. At this rate there would be a will without a motive.[100]

70. A will without motive (such as superficial reasonings suppose to be in God) I compared to Epicurus' chance. The author answers that Epicurus' chance is a blind necessity and not a choice of will. I reply that Epicurus' chance is not a necessity but something indifferent. Epicurus brought it in on purpose to avoid necessity. It is true that chance is blind, but a will without motive would be no less blind and no less owing to mere chance.

To Section 19

71. The author repeats here what has been already refuted above, no. 21, that matter cannot be created without God's choosing among indiscernibles. He would be in the right if matter consisted of atoms, similar particles, or other comparable fictions of superficial philosophy. But that great principle which proves there is no choice among indiscernibles also destroys these ill-contrived fictions.

To Section 20

72. The author objected against me in his *Third Reply* (nos. 7 and 8) that God would not have in himself a principle of acting, if he was determined by external things. I answered that the ideas of external things are in him and that therefore he is determined by internal reasons, that is, by his wisdom. But the author here will not understand to what end I said it.

To Section 21

73. He frequently confounds in his objections against me what God will not do with what he cannot do. See above, no. 9 <and below no. 76>. For example, God can do everything that is possible, but he will do only what is best. And therefore I do not say, as the author here will have it,

100. See Appendix A, no. 4.

that God cannot limit the extension of matter, but it is likely he will not do it and that he has thought it better to set no bounds to matter.

74. From extension to duration, *non valet consequentia.*[101] Though the extension of matter was unlimited, yet it would not follow that its duration would be also unlimited; no, even in the direction of the past it would not follow that it had no beginning. If it is the nature of things in the whole to grow uniformly in perfection, the universe of creatures must have had a beginning. And therefore there will be reasons to limit the duration of things, even though there were none to limit their extension. Besides, the world's having a beginning does not derogate from the infinity of its duration *a parte post*, or in the direction of the future, but bounds of the universe would derogate from the infinity of its extension. And therefore it is more reasonable to admit a beginning of the world than to admit any bounds of it, that the character of its infinite author may be preserved in both respects.

75. However, those who have admitted the eternity of the world or, at least (as some famous theologians have done), the possibility of its eternity, did not for all that deny its dependence on God, as the author here lays to their charge without any ground.

To Sections 22 and 23

76. He here further objects, without any reason, that according to my opinion whatever God can do, he must necessarily have done—as if he was ignorant that I have solidly confuted this notion in my *Theodicy* and that I have overthrown the opinion of those who maintain that there is nothing possible but what really happens, as some ancient philosophers did, and among others Diodorus in Cicero.[102] The author confounds moral necessity, which proceeds from the choice of what is best, with absolute necessity; he confounds the will of God with his power. God can produce everything that is possible or whatever does not imply a contradiction, but he wills only to produce what is the best among things possible. See what has been said above, no. 9 <and no. 74>.

77. God is not therefore a necessary agent in producing creatures, since he acts with choice. However, what the author adds here is ill grounded, namely, that a necessary agent would not be an agent at all. He frequently affirms things boldly and without any ground, advancing <against me> notions which cannot be proved.

---

101. "The inference is not valid."
102. Cicero, *De Fato*, chap. 17.

To Sections 24–28

78. The author alleges that it was not affirmed that space is "God's sensorium," but only "as it were his sensorium." The latter seems to be as improper and as little intelligible as the former.

To Section 29

79. Space is not the place of all things, for it is not the place of God. Otherwise there would be a thing coeternal with God and independent of him; no, he himself would depend on it, if he has need of place.

80. Nor do I see how it can be said that space is the place of ideas, for ideas are in the understanding.

81. It is also very strange to say that the soul of man is the soul of the images it possesses. The images, which are in the understanding, are in the mind, but if the mind was the soul of the images, they would then be extrinsic to it. And if the author means corporeal images, how then will he have a human mind be the soul of those images, since they are only transient impressions in a body belonging to that soul?

82. If it is by means of a sensorium that God perceives what passes in the world, it seems that things act on him and that therefore he is what we mean by a soul of the world. The author charges me with repeating objections without taking notice of the answers, but I do not see that he has answered this difficulty. They had better wholly lay aside this pretended sensorium.

To Section 30

83. The author speaks as if he did not understand how, according to my opinion, the soul is a representative principle. This is as if he had never heard of my pre-established harmony.[103]

84. I do not assent to the vulgar notions that the images of things are conveyed by the organs (of sense) to the soul. For it is not conceivable by what passage, or by what means of conveyance, these images can be carried from the organ to the soul. This vulgar notion in philosophy is not intelligible, as the new Cartesians have sufficiently shown. It cannot be explained how immaterial substance is affected by matter, and to maintain an unintelligible notion about this is having recourse to the scholastic chimerical notion of I-know-not-what inexplicable intentional species,[104]

103. See Appendix A, no. 5.

104. In scholastic doctrine intentional or intelligible species (*species intentionales*, as Clarke has it) were used to explain sense perception; see, for example, Thomas Aquinas, *Summa Theologiae* I, quest. 85, art. 2.

passing from the organs to the soul. Those Cartesians saw the difficulty, but they could not explain it. They had recourse to a <very particular> concourse of God, which would really be miraculous. But I think I have given the true solution of that enigma.

85. To say that God discerns what passes in the world because he is present to the things, and not by <the dependence on him of the continuation of their existence, which may be said to involve> a continual production of them, is saying something unintelligible. A mere presence or proximity of coexistence is not sufficient to make us understand how that which passes in one being should answer to what passes in another.

86. Besides, this is exactly falling into that opinion that makes God be the soul of the world, seeing it supposes God to perceive things, not by their dependence on him, that is, by a continual production of what is good and perfect in them, but by a kind of perception, such as that by which men fancy our soul perceives what passes in the body. This is a degrading of God's knowledge very much.

87. In truth and reality, this way of perception is wholly chimerical and has no place even in human souls. They perceive what passes outside them by what passes within them, answering to the things outside, in virtue of the harmony God has pre-established by the most beautiful and most admirable of all his productions,[105] by which every simple substance is by its nature (if one may so say) a concentration[106] and a living mirror of the whole universe according to its point of view.[107] This is likewise one of the most beautiful and most undeniable proofs of the existence of God, since none but God, namely, the universal cause, can produce such a harmony of things. But God himself cannot perceive things by the same means by which he makes other beings perceive them. He perceives them because he is able to produce that means. And other beings would not be caused to perceive them, if he himself did not produce them all harmonious and had not therefore in himself a representation of them—not as if that representation came from the things, but because the things proceed from him and because he is the efficient and exemplary cause of them. He perceives them because they proceed from him, if one may be allowed to say that he perceives them, which ought not to be said unless we divest that word of its imperfection, for else it seems to signify that things act on him. They exist and are known to him because he understands and wills them, and because what he wills is the

105. See Appendix A, no. 5.
106. See Appendix A, no. 2.
107. See Appendix A, no. 11.

same as what exists. The appears so much the more because he makes them be perceived by one another and makes them perceive one another in consequence of the natures he has given them once for all and which he keeps up only according to the laws of every one of them severally, which, though different one from another, yet terminate in an exact correspondence of the results of the whole. This surpasses all the ideas men have generally framed concerning the divine perfections and the works of God and raises [our notion of][108] them to the highest degree, as Mr. Bayle has acknowledged,[109] although he believed without any ground that it exceeded possibility.

88. To infer from that passage of Holy Scripture, in which God is said to have rested from his works, that there is no longer a continual production of them would be to make a very ill use of that text. It is true that there is no production of new simple substances, but it would be wrong to infer from this that God is now in the world only as the soul is conceived to be in the body, governing it merely by his presence without any concourse being necessary to continue its existence.

To Section 31

89. The harmony or correspondence between the soul and the body is not a perpetual miracle, but the effect or consequence of an original miracle worked at the creation of things, as all natural things are. Though indeed it is a perpetual wonder, as many natural things are.

90. The word *pre-established harmony* is a term of art, I confess, but it is not a term that explains nothing, since it is explained very intelligibly; and the author advances nothing that shows there is any difficulty in it.

91. The nature of every simple substance,[110] soul, or true monad being such that its following state is a consequence of the preceding one, here now is the cause of the harmony found out. For God needs only to make a simple substance become once and from the beginning a representation of the universe according to its point of view,[111] since from this alone it follows that it will be so perpetually, and that all simple substances will always have a harmony among themselves because they always represent the same universe.

108. Clarke's addition.

109. This most likely refers to the article "Rorarius," in Pierre Bayle, *Historical and Critical Dictionary* (2nd ed. 1702).

110. See Appendix A, no. 2.

111. See Appendix A, no. 11.

To Section 32

92. It is true that according to me the soul[112] does not disturb the laws of the body, nor the body those of the soul, and that the soul and body do only agree together, the one acting freely according to the rules of final causes and the other acting mechanically[113] according to the laws of efficient causes. But this does not derogate from the liberty of our souls, as the author here will have it. For every agent who acts according to final causes is free, although it happens to agree with an agent acting only by efficient causes without knowledge, or mechanically, because God, foreseeing what the free cause would do, did from the beginning regulate the machine in such manner that it cannot fail to agree with that free cause. Mr. Jaquelot[114] has very well resolved this difficulty in one of his books against Mr. Bayle, and I have cited the passage in my *Theodicy*, Part I, sec. 63. I shall speak of it again below, no. 124.

To Section 33

93. I do not admit that every action gives a new force to the patient. It frequently happens in the concourse of bodies that each of them preserves its force, as when two equal hard bodies meet directly. Then the direction only is changed without any change in the force, each of the bodies receiving the direction of the other and going back with the same speed it came.

94. However, I am far from saying that it is supernatural to give a new force to a body, for I acknowledge that one body does frequently receive a new force from another, which loses as much of its own. But I say only that it is supernatural that the whole universe of bodies should receive a new force, and consequently that one body should acquire any new force without the loss of as much in others. And therefore I say likewise that it is an indefensible opinion to suppose the soul gives force to the body, for then the whole universe of bodies would receive a new force.

95. The author's dilemma here is ill grounded, namely, that according to me, either a man must act supernaturally or be a mere machine like a watch. For man does not act supernaturally, and his body is truly a machine acting only mechanically, and yet his soul is a free cause.

112. See Appendix A, no. 5.
113. See Appendix A, no. 13.
114. Isaac Jaquelot, *Conformité de la Foi avec la Raison* (Amsterdam, 1705).

To Sections 34 and 35

96. I here refer to what has been or shall be said in this letter, no. 82, 86, and 111, concerning the comparison between God and a soul of the world, and how the opinion contrary to mine brings the one of these too near to the other.

To Section 36

97. I here also refer to what I have before said concerning the harmony between the soul and the body, no. 89, etc.

To Section 37

98. The author tells us that the soul is not in the brain but in the sensorium, without saying what that sensorium is. But supposing that sensorium to be extended, as I believe the author understands it, the same difficulty still remains, and the question returns whether the soul is diffused through that whole extension, great or small. For more or less in size is nothing to the purpose here.

To Section 38

99. I do not undertake here to establish my *Dynamics* or my doctrine of forces; this would not be a proper place for it. However, I can very well answer the objection here brought against me. I have affirmed that active forces are preserved in the world[115] [without diminutions][116]. The author objects that two soft or inelastic bodies meeting together lose some of their force. I answer, no. It is true that their wholes lose it with respect to their total motion, but their parts receive it, being shaken by the force of the concourse or shock. And therefore that loss of force is only in appearance. The forces are not destroyed but scattered among the small parts. The bodies do not lose their forces, but the case here is the same as when men change great money into small. However, I agree that the quantity of motion does not remain the same, and in this I approve what Sir Isaac Newton says, p. 341 of his *Optics*,[117] which the author here quotes. But I have shown elsewhere that there is a difference between the quantity of motion and the quantity of force.

115. Clarke refers to the footnote in sec. 13 of his *Third Reply*.
116. Clarke's addition.
117. See Appendix B, no. 3.

To Section 39

100. The author maintained against me that force does naturally lessen in the material universe, and that this arises from the dependence of things. (*Third Reply*, sec. 13 and 14.) In my third answer,[118] I asked him to prove that this imperfection is a consequence of the dependence of things. He avoids answering my demand by falling upon an incident and denying this to be an imperfection. But whether it is an imperfection or not, he should have proved that it is a consequence of the dependence of things.

101. However, that which would make the machine of the world as imperfect as that of an unskillful watchmaker surely must necessarily be an imperfection.

102. The author says now that it is a consequence of the inertia of matter. But this also he will not prove. That inertia, advanced here by him, mentioned by Kepler, repeated by Descartes <in his letters>, and made use of by me in my *Theodicy* in order to give a notion <and at the same time an example> of the natural imperfection of creatures, has no other effect than to make the velocities diminish when the quantities of matter are increased; but this is without any diminution of the forces.

To Section 40

103. I maintained that the dependence of the machine of the world on its divine author is rather a reason why there can be no such imperfection in it, and that the work of God does not need to be set right again, that it is not liable to be disordered, and lastly that it cannot lessen in perfection. Let anyone guess now how the author can hence infer against me, as he does, that if this is the case, then the material world must be infinite and eternal, without any beginning, and that God must always have created as many men and other kinds of creatures as can possibly be created.

To Section 41

104. I do not say that space is an order or situation which makes things capable of being situated; this would be nonsense. Anyone needs only consider my own words and add them to what I said above (no. 47), in order to show how the mind comes to form to itself an idea of space, and yet that there need not be any real and absolute being answering to that idea distinct from the mind and from all relations. I do not say, therefore, that space is an order or situation, but an order of situations, or (an order) according to which situations are disposed, and that abstract space is that

118. That is, Leibniz's *Fourth Letter* in this collection.

order of situations when they are conceived as being possible. Space is therefore something [merely][119] ideal. But it seems the author will not understand me. I have already answered the objection in this paper (no. 54) that order is not capable of quantity.

105. The author objects here that time cannot be an order of successive things because the quantity of time may become greater or less, and yet the order of successions continues the same. I answer that this is not so. For if the time is greater, there will be more successive and like states interposed, and if it is less, there will be fewer, seeing there is no vacuum, nor condensation, or penetration (if I may so speak), in times any more than in places.

106. It is true that the immensity and eternity of God would subsist though there were no creatures, but those attributes would have no dependence either on times or places. If there were no creatures, there would be neither time nor place, and consequently no actual space. The immensity of God is independent of space as his eternity is independent of time. These attributes signify only <with regard to these two orders of things> that God would be present and coexistent with all the things that should exist. And therefore I do not admit what is here advanced, that if God existed alone, there would be time and space as there is now, whereas then, in my opinion, they would be only in the ideas of God as mere possibilities. The immensity and eternity of God are things more transcendent than the duration and extension of creatures, not only with respect to the greatness, but also to the nature of the things. Those divine attributes do not imply the supposition of things extrinsic to God, such as are actual places and times. These truths have been sufficiently acknowledged by theologians and philosophers.

To Section 42

107. I maintained that an operation of God by which he should mend the machine of the material world,[120] tending in its nature (as this author claims) to lose all its motion, would be a miracle. His answer was that it would not be a miraculous operation because it would be usual and must frequently happen. I replied that it is not usualness or unusualness that makes a miracle properly so called, or a miracle of the highest sort, but it is surpassing the powers of creatures, and this is the [general][121] opinion of theologians and philosophers; and that therefore the author acknowledges at least that the thing he introduces and I disallow is, according to

---

119. Clarke's addition.
120. Clarke refers to his footnote in sec. 13 of his *Third Reply*.
121. Clarke's addition.

the received notion, a miracle of the highest sort, that is, one which surpasses all created powers, and that this is the very thing which all men
endeavor to avoid in philosophy. He answers now that this is appealing
from reason to vulgar opinion. But I reply again that this vulgar opinion,
according to which we ought in philosophy to avoid as much as possible
what surpasses the natures of creatures, is a very reasonable opinion. Otherwise nothing will be easier than to account for anything by bringing in
the deity, *Deum ex machina*, without minding the natures of things.

108. Besides, the common opinion of theologians ought not to be
looked upon merely as vulgar opinion. A man should have weighty reasons before he ventures to contradict it, and I see no such reasons here.

109. The author seems to depart from his own notion, according to
which a miracle ought to be unusual, when, in sec. 31, he objects to me
(though without any ground) that the pre-established harmony would be
a perpetual miracle. Here I say he seems to depart from his own notion,
unless he had a mind to argue against me *ad hominem*.

To Section 43

110. If a miracle differs from what is natural only in appearance and
with respect to us, so that we call only a miracle that which we seldom see,
there will be no internal real difference between a miracle and what is natural, and at the bottom everything will be either equally natural or equally
miraculous. Will theologians have reason to accept the former or philosophers the latter?

111. Will not this doctrine, moreover, tend to make God the soul of the
world, if all his operations are natural like those of our souls on our bodies? And so God will be a part of nature.

112. In good philosophy and sound theology we ought to distinguish
between what is explicable by the natures and powers of creatures and
what is explicable only by the powers of the infinite substance. We ought
to make an infinite difference between the operation of God, which goes
beyond the extent of natural powers, and the operations of things that follow the law God has given them, and which he has enabled them to follow
by their natural powers, though not without his assistance.

113. This overthrows attractions,[122] properly so called, and other operations inexplicable by the natural powers of creatures; those who assert
these kinds of operations must suppose them to be effected by miracles,
or else they have recourse to absurdities, that is, to the occult qualities of
the schools, which some men begin to revive under the specious name of

122. See Appendix A, no. 8.

forces, but which bring us back again into the kingdom of darkness. This is *inventa fruge, glandibus vesci.*[123]

114. In the time of Mr. Boyle and other excellent men who flourished in England under Charles II <in the early part of his reign>, nobody would have ventured to publish such chimerical notions. I hope that happy time will return under so good a government as the present <and that minds a little too much distracted by the misfortunes of the times will return to cultivate sound knowledge better>. Mr. Boyle made it his chief business to inculcate that everything was done mechanically in natural philosophy. But it is men's misfortune to grow disgusted in the end with reason itself and to be weary of light. Chimeras begin to appear again, and they are pleasing because they have something in them that is wonderful. What has happened in poetry happens also in the philosophical world. People have grown weary of rational romances, such as were the French *Clélie* or the German *Aramena*;[124] and they have become fond again of the tales of fairies.

115. As for the motions of the celestial bodies, and even the formation of plants and animals, there is nothing in them that looks like a miracle except their beginning. The organism of animals is a mechanism that supposes a divine preformation. What follows upon it is purely natural and entirely mechanical.

116. Whatever is performed in the body of man and of every animal[125] is no less mechanical than what is performed in a watch. The difference is only such as ought to be between a machine of divine invention and the workmanship of such a limited artist as man is.

To Section 44

117. There is no difficulty among theologians about the miracles of angels. The question is only about the use of that word. It may be said that angels work miracles, but less properly so called or of an inferior order. To dispute about this would be a mere question about a word. It may be said that the angel who carried Habakkuk through the air, and he who troubled the water of the pool of Bethesda worked a miracle. But it was not a miracle of the highest order, for it may be explained by the natural powers of angels, which surpass those of man.

---

123. "To feed on acorns when corn has been discovered."

124. *Clélie* (1656) is a six-volume novel by Mlle de Scudery; *Aramena* (1666–1673) is a five-volume novel by Duke Anton Ulrich of Brunsvick-Wolfenbüttel.

125. See Appendix A, no. 13.

To Section 45

118. I objected that an attraction properly so called, or in the scholastic sense, would be an operation at a distance without any means intervening. The author answers here that an attraction without any means intervening would indeed be a contradiction. Very well! But then what does he mean when he will have the sun attract the globe of the earth through an empty space? Is it God himself that performs it? But this would be a miracle if ever there was any. This would surely exceed the powers of creatures.

119. Or are perhaps some immaterial substances or some spiritual rays, or some accident without a substance, or some kind of intentional species, or some other I-know-not-what, the means by which this is claimed to be performed? Of these sorts of things the author seems to have still a good stock in his head, without explaining himself sufficiently.

120. That means of communication (he says) is invisible, intangible, not mechanical. He might as well have added inexplicable, unintelligible, precarious, groundless, and unprecedented.

121. But it is regular (the author says), it is constant, and consequently natural. I answer that it cannot be regular without being reasonable, nor natural unless it can be explained by the natures of creatures.

122. If the means which causes an attraction properly so called are constant and at the same time inexplicable by the powers of creatures, and yet are true, it must be a perpetual miracle, and if it is not miraculous, it is false. It is a chimerical thing, a scholastic occult quality.

123. The case would be the same as in a body going around without receding in the tangent, although nothing that can be explained hindered it from receding. This is an instance I have already advanced, and the author has not thought fit to answer it because it shows too clearly the difference between what is truly natural, on the one side, and a chimerical occult quality of the schools, on the other.

To Section 46

124. All the natural forces of bodies are subject to mechanical laws, and all the natural powers of spirits are subject to moral laws. The former follow the order of efficient causes, and the latter follow the order of final causes. The former operate without liberty, like a watch; the latter operate with liberty, though they exactly agree with that machine which another cause, free and superior, has adapted to them beforehand. I have already spoken of this above, no. 92.

125. I shall conclude with what the author objected against me at the beginning of this *Fourth Reply*, to which I have already given an answer above (no. 18, 19, 20). But I deferred speaking more fully on that matter

to the conclusion of this paper. He claimed that I have been guilty of a petition of principle.[126] But of what principle, I beseech you? Would to God less clear principles had never been laid down. The principle in question is the principle of the need for a sufficient reason for anything to exist, for any event to happen, for any truth to take place. Is this a principle that needs to be proved? The author granted it or pretended to grant it, no. 2 of his *Third Reply*; possibly because the denial of it would have appeared too unreasonable. But either he has done it only in words or he contradicts himself or retracts his concession.

126. I dare say that without this great principle one cannot prove the existence of God nor account for many other important truths.

127. Has not everybody made use of this principle on a thousand occasions? It is true that it has been neglected out of carelessness on many occasions, but that neglect has been the true cause of chimeras, such as are (for instance) an absolute real time or space, a vacuum, atoms, attraction in the scholastic sense, a physical influence of the soul over the body <and of the body over the soul>, and a thousand other fictions either derived from erroneous opinions of the ancients or lately invented by modern philosophers.

128. Was it not on account of Epicurus' violating this great principle that the ancients derided his groundless declination of atoms? And I dare say that the scholastic attraction, revived in our days and no less derided about thirty years ago, is not at all more reasonable.

129. I have often defied people to advance an instance against that great principle, to bring any one uncontested example in which it fails. But they have never done it, nor ever will. It is certain that there is an infinite number of instances in which it succeeds, <or rather it succeeds> in all the known cases in which it has been made use of. From this one may reasonably judge that it will succeed also in unknown cases or in such cases as can only by its means become known, according to the method of experimental philosophy, which proceeds *a posteriori;* although the principle was not perhaps otherwise justified by pure reason, or *a priori.*

130. To deny this great principle is likewise to do as Epicurus did, who was reduced to deny that other great principle, namely, the principle of contradiction, which is that every intelligible enunciation must be either true or false. Chrysippus undertook to prove that principle against Epicurus, but I think I need not imitate him. I have already said what is sufficient to justify mine, and I might say something more on it, but perhaps it would be too abstruse for this present dispute. And I believe reasonable

126. That is, a begging of the question.

and impartial men will grant me that having forced an adversary to deny
that principle is reducing him *ad absurdum.*

Clarke's Fifth Reply[127]

As multitudes of words are neither an argument of clear ideas in the
writer nor a proper means of conveying clear notions to the reader, I shall
endeavor to give a distinct answer to this *Fifth Letter,* as briefly as I can.
    1–20. There is no (sec. 3) similitude between a balance being moved by
weights or impulse and a mind moving itself or acting on the view of certain motives. The difference is that the one is entirely passive, which is
being subject to absolute necessity, the other not only is acted on but also
acts, which is the essence of liberty. To (sec. 14) suppose that an equal
apparent goodness in different ways of acting takes away from the mind[128]
all power of acting at all, as an equality of weights keeps a balance necessarily at rest, is denying the mind to have in itself a principle of action,
and is confounding the power of acting with the impression made on the
mind by the motive, in which the mind is purely passive. The motive, or
thing considered as in view, is something extrinsic to the mind. The
impression made on the mind by that motive is the perceptive quality in
which the mind is passive. The doing of anything, upon and after or in
consequence of that perception, is the power of self-motion or action,
which in all animate agents is spontaneity and in moral agents is what we
properly call liberty. Not carefully distinguishing these things, but confounding (sec. 15) the motive with the principle of action and denying the
mind to have any principle of action besides the motive (when indeed, in
receiving the impression of the motive, the mind is purely passive), this, I
say, is the ground of the whole error, and leads men to think that the mind
is no more active than a balance would be with the addition of a power of
perception, which is wholly taking away the very notion of liberty. A balance pushed on both sides with equal force, or pressed on both sides with
equal weights, cannot move at all; and supposing the balance endowed
with a power of perception so as to be sensible of its own incapacity to
move, or so as to deceive itself[129] with an imagination that it moves itself
when indeed it is only moved, it would be exactly in the same state in
which this learned author supposes a free agent to be in all cases of absolute indifference. But the fallacy plainly lies here: the balance, for lack of
having in itself a principle or power of action, cannot move at all when the

127. October 29, 1716. Leibniz died on November 14, 1716.
128. See Appendix A, no. 4.
129. See Appendix A, no. 12.

weights are equal, but a free agent, when there appear two or more perfectly similar reasonable ways of acting, has still within itself, by virtue of its self-motive principle, a power of acting, and it may have very strong and good reasons not to forbear acting at all, when yet there may be no possible reason to determine one particular way of doing the thing to be better than another. To affirm therefore (sec. 16–19, 69) that, supposing two different ways of placing certain particles of matter were equally good and reasonable, God could neither wisely nor possibly place them in either of those ways, for lack of a sufficient weight to determine him which way he should choose, is making God not an active but a passive being—which is not to be a God or governor at all. And for denying the possibility of the supposition that there may be two equal parts of matter which may with equal fitness be transposed in situation, no other reason can be advanced but this (sec. 20) *petitio principii*, that then this learned writer's notion of a sufficient reason would not be well-grounded. For otherwise how can any man say that it is (sec. 16, 17, 69, 66) impossible for God to have wise and good reasons to create many particles of matter exactly alike in different parts of the universe? In this case, the parts of space being alike, it is evident there can be no reason, but mere will, for not having originally transposed their situations. And yet even this cannot be reasonably said to be a (sec. 16, 69) will without motive, for as much as the wise reasons God may possibly have to create many particles of matter exactly alike must consequently be a motive to him to take (what a balance could not do) one out of two absolutely indifferents, that is, to place them in one situation, when the transposing of them could not but have been exactly alike good.

Necessity, in philosophical questions, always signifies absolute necessity (sec. 4–13). *Hypothetical necessity*[130] and *moral necessity* are only figurative ways of speaking and, in philosophical strictness of truth, are no necessity at all. The question is not whether a thing must be, when it is supposed that it is or that it is to be (which is hypothetical necessity); neither is it the question whether it is true that a good being continuing to be good cannot do evil, or a wise being continuing to be wise cannot act unwisely, or a veracious person continuing to be veracious cannot tell a lie (which is moral necessity). But the true and only question in philosophy concerning liberty is whether the immediate physical cause or principle of action is indeed in him whom we call the agent, or whether it is some other sufficient reason, which is the real cause of the action by operating on the agent and making him be, not indeed an agent, but a mere patient.

130. Clarke refers to his "Sermons at Mr. Boyle's Lecture," Part I, p. 106 (4th ed.); *Works*, vol. 2, p. 566.

It may here be observed, by the way, that this learned author contradicts his own hypothesis when he says that (sec. 11) the will does not always precisely follow the practical understanding, because it may sometimes find reasons to suspend its resolution. For are not those very reasons the last judgment of the practical understanding?

21–25. If it is possible for God to make or to have made two pieces of matter exactly alike, so that transposing them in situation would be perfectly indifferent, this learned author's notion of a sufficient reason falls to the ground. To this he answers not (as his argument requires) that it is impossible for God to make two pieces exactly alike,[131] but that it is not wise for him to do so. But how does he know that it would not be wise for God to do so? Can he prove that it is not possible that God may have wise reasons for creating many parts of matter exactly alike in different parts of the universe? The only argument he advances is that then there would not be a sufficient reason to determine the will of God as to which piece should be placed in which situation. But if, in case anything else should appear to the contrary, God may possibly have many wise reasons for creating many pieces exactly alike, will the indifference alone of the situation of such pieces make it impossible that he should create or impossible that it should be wise in him to create them? I humbly conceive that this is an (sec. 20) express begging of the question. To the like argument drawn by me from the absolute indifference of the original particular determination of motion, no answer has been returned.

26–32. In these articles there seem to be contained many contradictions. It is allowed (sec. 26) that two things exactly alike would really be two, and yet it is still adduced that they would need the *principle of individuation*, and in the *Fourth Letter*, sec. 6, it was expressly affirmed that they would be only the same thing under two names. A (sec. 26) supposition is allowed to be possible, and yet I must not be allowed to make the supposition. The (sec. 27) parts of time and space are allowed to be exactly alike in themselves, but not so when bodies exist in them. Different coexistent parts of space and different successive parts of time are (sec. 28) compared to a straight line cutting another straight line in two coincident points, which are but one point only. It is affirmed that (sec. 29) space is nothing but the order of things coexisting, and yet it is (sec. 30) confessed that the material universe may possibly be finite, in which case there must necessarily be an empty extramundane space. It is (sec. 30, 8, 73) allowed that God could make the material universe finite, and yet supposing it to be possibly finite is called not only a unreasonable supposition, void of design, but also an (sec. 29) impracticable fiction, and it is affirmed that

131. See Leibniz's *Fourth Letter*, sec. 2, 3, 6, 13, and 15.

there can be no possible reason which can limit the quantity of matter.[132] It is affirmed that the motion of the material universe would produce (sec. 29) no change at all, and yet no answer is given to the argument I advanced that a sudden increase or stoppage of the motion of the whole would give a sensible shock to all the parts, and it is as evident that a circular motion of the whole[133] would produce a *vis centrifuga*[134] in all the parts. My argument that the material world must be movable, if the whole is finite, is (sec. 31) denied because the parts of space are immovable, of which the whole is infinite and necessarily existing. It is affirmed that motion necessarily implies a (sec. 31) relative change of situation in one body with regard to other bodies, and yet no way is shown to avoid this absurd consequence that then the mobility of one body depends on the existence of other bodies, and that any single body existing alone would be incapable of motion, or that the parts of a circulating body (suppose the sun) would lose the *vis centrifuga* arising from their circular motion, if all the extrinsic matter around them was annihilated. Lastly, it is affirmed that the (sec. 32) infinity of matter is an effect of the will of God, and yet Descartes' notion is (ibid.) approved as irrefutable; the only foundation of this all men know to have been the supposition that matter was infinite necessarily in the nature of things, since it is a contradiction to suppose it finite. His words are "Puto implicare contradictionem, ut mundus finitus,"[135] which, if it is true, it never was in the power of God to determine the quantity of matter, and consequently he neither was the creator of it nor can destroy it.

And indeed there seems to run a continual inconsistency through the whole of what this learned author writes concerning matter and space. For sometimes he argues against a vacuum (or space void of matter) as if it was (sec. 29, 33–5, 62–3) absolutely impossible in the nature of things, space and matter being (sec. 62) inseparable, and yet frequently he allows the quantity of matter in the universe to depend upon the (sec. 30, 32, 73) will of God.

33–35. To the argument drawn against a plenum of matter from the lack of resistance in certain spaces, this learned author answers that those spaces are filled with a matter which has no (sec. 35) gravity. But the argument was not drawn from gravity, but from resistance, which must be

---

132. *Fourth Letter*, sec. 21.

133. See Appendix A, no. 10.

134. "Centrifugal force."

135. *To More*, April 15, 1649, *Oeuvres de Descartes*, eds. Charles Adam and Paul Tannery (2nd ed., Paris: Vrin, 1964–1974), vol. V, p. 345: "I think it implies a contradiction that the world should be finite."

proportional to the quantity of matter, whether the matter had any gravity or not.[136]

To obviate this reply, he claims that (sec. 34) resistance does not arise so much from the quantity of matter as from its difficulty of giving place. But this allegation is wholly wide of the purpose, because the question related only to such fluid bodies which have little or no tenacity, as water and quicksilver whose parts have no other difficulty of giving place but what arises from the quantity of the matter they contain. The instance of a (ibid.) floating piece of wood containing less of heavy matter than an equal bulk of water, and yet making greater resistance, is wonderfully unphilo- sophical, for an equal bulk of water shut up in a vessel, or frozen into ice and floating, makes a greater resistance than the floating wood, the resis- tance then arising from the whole bulk of the water; but when the water is loose and at liberty in its state of fluidity, the resistance is then not made by the whole, but by part only of the equal bulk of water, and then it is no wonder that it seems to make less resistance than the wood.

36–48. These paragraphs do not seem to contain serious arguments, but only represent in an ill light the notion of the immensity or omnipres- ence of God, who is not a mere *intelligentia supramundana* (semota a nos- tris rebus sejunctaque longe),[137] and who "is not far from everyone of us, for in him we" (and all things) "live and move and have our being."[138]

The space occupied by a body is not the (sec. 36, 37) extension of the body, but the extended body exists in that space.

There is no such thing in reality as (sec. 38) bounded space, but only we in our imagination fix our attention on what part or quantity we please of that which itself is always and necessarily unbounded.

Space is not an (sec. 39) affection of one body or of another body or of any finite being, nor passes from subject to subject, but is always invari- ably the immensity of one only and always the same *immensum*.

Finite spaces are not at all the (sec. 40) affections of finite substances, but they are only those parts of infinite space in which finite substances exist.

If matter was infinite, still infinite space would no more be an (sec. 41) affection of that infinite body than finite spaces are the affections of finite bodies, but in that case the infinite matter would be, as finite bodies now are, in the infinite space.

Immensity as well as eternity is (sec. 42) essential to God. The parts of

136. Clarke adds: "Otherwise, what makes the body of the earth more difficult to be moved (even the same way that its gravity tends) than the smallest ball?"

137. "Remote from us and greatly separated from things."

138. Acts 17.27–8.

immensity[139] (being totally of a different kind from corporeal, partable, separable, divisible, movable parts, which are the ground of corruptibility) do no more hinder immensity from being essentially one than the parts of duration hinder eternity from being essentially one.

God himself suffers no (sec. 43) change at all by the variety and changeableness of things which live and move and have their being in him.

This (sec. 44) strange doctrine is the express assertion of Saint Paul[140] as well as the plain voice of nature and reason.

God does not exist (sec. 45) in space and in time, but his existence[141] causes space and time. And when, according to the analogy of vulgar speech, we say that he exists in all space and in all time, the words mean only that he is omnipresent and eternal, that is, that boundless space and time are necessary consequences of his existence, and not that space and time are beings distinct from him and in which he exists.

How[142] (sec. 46) finite space is not the extension of bodies, I have shown just above, in sec. 40. And the two following sections also (sec. 47

---

139. Clarke refers to his *Third Reply*, sec. 3, and *Fourth Reply*, sec. 11.

140. Acts 17.27–8.

141. Clarke refers to the footnote in sec. 10 of his *Fourth Reply*.

142. Clarke notes: The principal occasion or reason of the confusion and inconsistencies, which appear in what most writers have advanced concerning the nature of space, seems to be that (unless they attend carefully) men are very apt to neglect that necessary distinction (without which there can be no clear reasoning) which ought always to be made between abstracts and concretes, such as are *immensitas* and *immensum*, and also between ideas and things, such as are the notion (which is within our own mind) of immensity and the real immensity actually existing outside us.

All the conceptions (I think) that ever have been or can be framed concerning space are these which follow: That it is either absolutely nothing or a mere idea or only a relation of one thing to another, or it is body or some other substance, or else a property of a substance

That it is not absolutely nothing is most evident. For of nothing there is no quantity no dimensions no properties. This principle is the first foundation of all science whatsoever, expressing the only difference between what does and what does not exist.

That it is not a mere idea is likewise most manifest. For no idea of space can possibly be framed larger than finite, and yet reason demonstrates that it is a contradiction for space itself not to be actually infinite.

That it is not a bare relation of one thing to another, arising from their situation or order among themselves, is no less apparent, because space is a quantity, which relations (such as situation and order) are not, as I have largely shown below,

and 48) need only to be compared with what has been already (see also
below, sec. 53 and 54) said.

49–51. These seem to me to be only a quibbling with words. Concerning the question about space having parts, see above, *Third Reply*, sec. 3,
and *Fourth Reply*, sec. 11.

52 and 53. My argument here for the notion of space being really independent of body is founded on the possibility of the material universe
being finite and movable; it is not enough therefore for this learned writer
to reply that he thinks it would not have been wise and reasonable for God
to have made the material universe finite and movable. He must either
affirm that it was impossible for God to make the material world finite and
movable, or else he must of necessity allow the strength of my argument
drawn from the possibility of the world's being finite and movable. Neither is it sufficient barely to repeat his assertion that the motion of a finite
material universe would be nothing and (for lack of other bodies to compare it with) would (sec. 52) produce no discoverable change, unless he
could disprove the instance I gave of a very great change that would happen, namely, that the parts would be sensibly shocked by a sudden accel-
eration or stopping of the motion of the whole—to which instance he has
not attempted to give any answer.

53. Whether this learned author's being forced here to acknowledge
the difference between absolute real motion and relative motion does not
necessarily infer that space is really a quite different thing from the situation or order of bodies, I leave to the judgment of those who shall be
pleased to compare what this learned writer here advances with what Sir
Isaac Newton has said in his *Principia* I, definition 8.[143]

54. I had adduced that time and space were **quantities**, which situation
and order were not. To this it is replied that order has its quantity, there is
that which goes before and that which follows, there is distance or interval.

---

in sec. 54. Also because, if the material universe is or can possibly be finite, there
cannot but be actual or possible extramundane space; see in sec. 31, 52, and 73.

   That space is not body is also most clear. For then body would be necessarily infinite and no space could be void of resistance to motion. This is contrary to
experience.

   That space is not any kind of substance is no less plain, because infinite
space is *immensitas*, not *immensum*, whereas infinite substance is *immensum* not *immensitas*—just as duration is not a substance, because infinite duration is *aeternitas*
not *aeternum*, but infinite substance *is aeternum* not *aeternitas*.

   It remains therefore, by necessary consequence, that space is a property, in
like manner as duration is. *Immensitas* is τoυ *immensi*, just as *aeternitas* is τoυ *aeterni*.

143. See Appendix B, no. 1.

I answer that going before and following constitutes situation or order, but the distance, interval, or quantity of time or space, in which one thing follows another, is entirely a distinct thing from the situation or order and does not constitute any quantity of situation or order; the situation or order may be the same when the quantity of time or space intervening is very different. This learned author further replies that ratios or proportions (sec. 54) have their quantity, and therefore so may time and space, though they are nothing but relations. I answer first that if it had been true that some particular sorts of relations, such as ratios or proportions were quantities, still it would not have followed that situation and order, which are relations of a quite different kind, would have been quantities too. But secondly, proportions are not quantities but the proportions of quantities. If they were quantities, they would be the quantities of quantities, which is absurd. Also, if they were quantities, they would (like all other quantities) always increase by addition, but the addition of the proportion of 1 to 1 to the proportion of 1 to 1 still makes no more than the proportion of 1 to 1, and the addition of the proportion of half to 1 to the proportion of 1 to 1 does not make the proportion of 1 and a half to 1, but the proportion only of half to 1. That which mathematicians sometimes inaccurately call the quantity of proportion is (accurately and strictly speaking) only the quantity of the relative or comparative magnitude of one thing with regard to another, and proportion is not the comparative magnitude itself, but the comparison or relation of the magnitude to another. The proportion of 6 to 1, with regard to that of 3 to 1, is not a double quantity of proportion, but the proportion of a double quantity. And, in general, what they call *bearing a greater or less proportion* is not bearing a greater or less quantity of proportion or relation, but bearing the proportion or relation of a greater or less quantity to another; it is not a greater or less quantity of comparison, but the comparison of a greater or less quantity. The (sec. 54) logarithmic expression of a proportion is not (as this learned author calls it) a measure, but only an artificial index or sign of proportion; it is not the expressing a quantity of proportion, but barely a denoting the number of times that any proportion is repeated or complicated. The logarithm of the proportion of equality is 0 and yet it is as real and as much a proportion as any other, and when the logarithm is negative, as $\overline{1}$, yet the proportion of which it is the sign or index is itself affirmative. Duplicate or triplicate proportion does not denote a double or triple quantity of proportion, but the number of times that the proportion is repeated. The tripling of any magnitude or quantity once produces a magnitude or quantity, which to the former bears the proportion of 3 to 1. The tripling it a second time produces (not a double quantity of proportion but) a magnitude or quantity, which to the former bears the proportion (called duplicate) of 9 to 1. The tripling it a third time produces (not a triple quantity of proportion but) a magnitude or quantity, which to the former bears the proportion (called triplicate) of 27 to 1, and so on. Thirdly, time and space are not of the nature of proportions at all, but of the nature of absolute quantities to which proportions belong. As for example, the proportion of 12 to 1 is a much greater proportion (that is, as I now observed, not a greater quantity of proportion, but the proportion of a greater comparative quantity) than that of 2 to 1, and yet one and the same unvaried quantity may to one thing bear the proportion of 12 to 1 and to another thing at the same time the proportion of 2 to 1. Thus the space of a day bears a much greater proportion to an hour than it does to half a day, and yet it remains, notwithstanding both the proportions, the same unvaried quantity of time. Time therefore (and space likewise by the same argument) is not of the nature of a proportion, but of an absolute and unvaried quantity to which different proportions belong. Unless this reasoning can be shown to be false, our learned author's opinion still remains by his own confession[144] a contradiction.

55–63. All this seems to me to be a plain contradiction, and I am willing to leave it to the judgment of the learned. In one paragraph (sec. 56) there is a plain and distinct supposition that the universe might be created as much sooner or later as God pleased. In the rest (sec. 55, 57–63) the very terms (sooner or later) are treated as unintelligible terms and impossible suppositions.[145] Similar things occur concerning the space in which matter subsists; see above, in sec. 26–32.

64 and 65. See above, in sec. 54.

66–70. See above, in sec. 1–20 and in sec. 21–25. I shall here only add that (sec. 70) comparing the will of God when it chooses one out of many equally good ways of acting to Epicurus' chance, who allowed no will no intelligence no active principle at all in the formation of the universe, is comparing together two things than which no two things can possibly be more different.

71. See above, in sec. 21–25.

72. See above, in sec. 1–20.

73–75. In the consideration whether space is independent of matter and whether the material universe can be finite and movable (see above, in sec. 120, and in 26–32), the question is not concerning the wisdom or (sec. 73) will of God, but concerning the absolute and necessary nature of things. If the material universe can possibly be finite and movable by the will of God (which this learned author here finds himself necessitated to grant, though he perpetually treats it as an impossible supposition), then

144. *Fourth Letter*, sec. 16.
145. *Fourth Letter*, sec. 15.

space (in which that motion is performed) is manifestly independent of matter. But if, on the contrary, the material universe cannot be finite and movable[146] and space cannot be independent of matter, then (I say) it follows evidently that God neither can nor ever could set bounds to matter, and consequently the material universe must be not only boundless, but (sec. 74) eternal also, both *a parte ante* and *a parte post*,[147] necessarily and independently of the will of God. For the opinion of those who contend that the world (sec. 75) might possibly be eternal by the will of God exercising his eternal power, this has no relation at all to the matter at present in question.

76 and 77. See above, in sec. 73–75, and in sec. 1–20, and below, in sec. 103.

78. This paragraph contains no new objection. The aptness and intelligibility of the similitude made use of by Sir Isaac Newton, and here excepted against, has been abundantly explained in the foregoing *Replies*.

79–82. All that is objected in the (sec. 79, 80) two former of these paragraphs is a mere quibbling with words. The existence of God (as has often been already observed) causes space, and in that space all other things exist. It is therefore (sec. 80) the place of ideas likewise, because it is the place of the substances themselves in whose understandings ideas exist.

The soul of man being (sec. 81) the soul of the images of the things it perceives was advanced by me, in way of comparison, as an instance of a ridiculous notion, and this learned writer pleasantly argues against it as if I had affirmed it to be my own opinion.

God perceives everything, not (sec. 82) by means of any organ, but by being himself actually present everywhere. This everywhere therefore, or universal space, is the place of his perception. The notion of *sensorium* and of the soul of the world has been abundantly explained before. It is too much to desire to have the conclusion given up without bringing any further objection against the premises.

83–88, and 89–91. That (sec. 83) the soul is a representative principle, that (sec. 87) every simple substance is by its nature a concentration and living mirror of the whole universe,[148] that (sec. 91) it is a representation of the universe according to its point of view,[149] and that all simple substances will always have a harmony between themselves because they always represent the same universe, all this, I acknowledge, I understand not at all.

146. *Fourth Letter*, sec. 21 and *Fifth Letter*, sec. 29.
147. "Both in the direction of the past and in the direction of the future."
148. See Appendix A, no. 2.
149. See Appendix A, no. 11.

Concerning the (sec. 83, 87, 89, 90) *harmonia praestabilita*,[150] by which the affections of the soul and the mechanic motions of the body are affirmed to agree without at all influencing each other,[151] see below, in sec. 110–116.

That the images of things are conveyed by the organs of sense into the sensory, where the soul perceives them, is affirmed but not proved to be an (sec. 84) unintelligible notion.

Concerning (sec. 84) immaterial substance affecting or being affected by material substance, see below, in sec. 110–116.

That God (sec. 85) perceives and knows all things not by being present to them, but by continually producing them anew, is a mere fiction of the schoolmen, without any proof.

The objection concerning God's being (sec. 86, 87, 88, 82) the soul of the world has been abundantly answered above, *Second Reply*, sec. 12, and *Fourth Reply*, sec. 32.

92. To suppose that all the motions of our bodies are necessary and caused entirely (sec. 92, 95, 116) by mere mechanical impulses of matter[152] altogether independent on the soul is what (I cannot but think) tends to introduce necessity and fate. It tends to make men be thought as mere machines, as Descartes imagined beasts to be, by taking away all arguments drawn from phenomena,[153] that is, from the actions of men, to prove that there is any soul, or anything more than mere matter in men at all. See below, in sec. 110–116.

93–95. I adduced that every action is the giving of a new force to the thing acted upon. To this it is objected that two equal hard bodies striking each other return with the same force, and that therefore their action on each other gives no new force. It might be sufficient to reply that the bodies do neither of them return with their own force, but each of them loses its own force and each returns with a new force impressed by the other's elasticity, for if they are not elastic, they do not return at all. But indeed, all mere mechanical communications of motion are not properly action, but mere passiveness, both in the bodies that impel and that are impelled. Action is the beginning of a motion where there was none before from a principle of life or activity, and if God or man or any living or active power ever influences anything in the material world, and everything is not mere absolute mechanism, there must be a continual increase and decrease of

150. "Pre-established harmony."
151. See Appendix A, no. 5.
152. See Appendix A, no. 13.
153. See Appendix A, no. 12.

the whole quantity of motion in the universe—which this learned gentleman[154] frequently denies.

154. Clarke notes: There appears a great confusion and inconsistency in Mr. Leibniz's whole notion of this matter. For the word *force,* and *active force,* signifies in the present question the impetus or relative impulsive force of bodies in motion; see my *Third Reply,* sec. 13. Mr. Leibniz constantly uses the word in this sense, as when he speaks (sec. 93, 94, 99, and 107 of this last answer) of bodies not changing their force after reflection because they return with the same speed; of a body's receiving a new force from another body which loses as much of its own; of the impossibility that one body should acquire any new force without the loss of as much in others; of the new force which the whole material universe would receive, if the soul of man communicated any force to the body; and of active forces continuing always the same in the universe because the force which inelastic bodies lose in their whole is communicated to and dispersed among their small parts. Now this impetus, or relative impulsive active force of bodies in motion, is evidently both in reason and experience always proportional to the quantity of motion. Therefore, according to Mr. Leibniz's principles, since this impulsive active force is always the same in quantity, the quantity of motion also must of necessity always be the same in the universe. Yet elsewhere he consistently acknowledges (sec. 99) that the quantity of motion is not always the same, and in the *Acta Eruditorum* of 1686, p. 161 [GM VI, 117–9], he endeavors to prove that the quantity of motion in the universe is not always the same, from that very argument, and from that single argument only (of the quantity of impulsive force being always the same) which, if it was true, would necessarily infer, on the contrary, that the quantity of motion could not but always be the same. The reason of his inconsistency in this matter was his computing, by a wonderfully unphilosophical error, the quantity of impulsive force in an ascending body from the quantity of its matter and of the space described by it in ascending, without considering the time of its ascending.

He says (*Acta Eruditorum,* 1686, p. 162): "I suppose the same force is required to raise a body A of one pound weight to the height of four yards which will raise the body B of four pounds weight to the height of one yard. This is granted both by the Cartesians and other philosophers and mathematicians of our times. And from this it follows that the body A, by falling from the height of four yards, acquires exactly the same force as the body B, by falling from the height of one yard."

But in this supposition Mr. Leibniz is greatly mistaken. Neither the Cartesians nor any other philosophers or mathematicians ever grant this, except in such cases only where the times of ascent or descent are equal. If a pendulum oscillates in a cycloid, the arch of the cycloid described in ascending will be as the force with which the pendulous body begins to ascend from the lowest point, because the times of ascending are equal. And if equal bodies librate upon the arm of a balance at various distances from the axis of the balance, the forces of the bodies will be in proportion as the arcs described by them in librating, because they librate in the same time. And if two equal globes lying upon an horizontal plane are impelled by unequal forces, they will in equal times describe spaces proportional to the forces impelling them. Or if unequal globes are impelled with equal forces, they will in equal times describe spaces reciprocally proportional to their masses. And in all these cases, if equal bodies are impelled by unequal forces, the forces impressed, the velocities generated, and the spaces described in equal times will be proportional to one another. And if the bodies are unequal, the velocity of the bigger bodies will be so much less as the bodies are bigger, and therefore the motion (arising from the mass and velocity together) will be in all these cases, and in all other cases consequently, proportional to the force impressed. (From this, by the way, it plainly follows that if there is always the same impulsive force in the world, as Mr. Leibniz affirms, there must be always the same motion in the world, contrary to what he affirms.)

But Mr. Leibniz confounds the cases where the times are equal with the cases where the times are unequal, and chiefly that of bodies rising and falling at the ends of the unequal arms of a balance *(Acta Eruditorum*, 1686, p. 162; 1690, p. 234; 1691, p. 439; 1695, p. 155 [GM VI, 117–9; 193–203, 204–11, 234]) is confounded by him with that of bodies falling downwards and thrown upwards without allowing for the inequality of the time. For a body with one and the same force and one and the same velocity will in a longer time describe a greater space, and therefore the time is to be considered and the forces are not to be reckoned proportional to the spaces, unless where the times are equal. Where the times are unequal, the forces of equal bodies are as the spaces applied to the times. And in this the Cartesians and other philosophers and mathematicians agree, all of them making the impulsive forces of bodies proportional to their motions, and measuring their motions by their masses and velocities together, and their velocities by the spaces which they describe, applied to the times in which they describe them. If a body thrown upwards does, by doubling its velocity, ascend four times higher in twice the time, its impulsive force will be increased, not in the proportion of the space described by its ascent, but in the proportion of that space applied to the time, that is, in the proportion of 4/2 to 1/1 or 2 to 1. For if, in this case, the force should be increased in the proportion of 4 to 1, and, in oscillating in a cycloid, the same body with the same velocity doubled describes only a doubled arc, and its force is therefore only doubled, this body, with one and the same degree of velocity, would have twice as much force when thrown upwards as when thrown horizontally—which is a plain contradiction. And there is the same contradiction in affirming that although a body at the end of the unequal arms of a balance, by doubling its velocity, acquires only a double impulsive force, yet, by being thrown upwards with the same doubled velocity, it acquires a quadruple impulsive force—in this assertion, I say, there is the same contradiction, for equal bodies with equal velocities cannot have unequal impulsive forces.

On the supposition of gravity being uniform, Galileo demonstrated the motion of projectiles in mediums void of resistance, and his propositions are allowed by all mathematicians, not excepting Mr. Leibniz himself. Now, supposing the time of a falling body to be divided into equal parts, since gravity is uniform, and, by being so, acts equally in equal parts of time, it must by its action impress and communicate to the falling body equal impulsive forces, velocities, and motions, in equal times. And therefore the impulsive force, the velocity, and the motion of the falling body will increase in proportion to the time of falling. But the space described by the falling body arises partly from the velocity of the body and partly from the time of its falling, and so is in a compound ratio of them both, or as the square of either of them, and consequently as the square of the impulsive force. And by the same way of arguing, it may be proved that when a body is thrown upwards with any impulsive force, the height to which it will ascend will be as the square of that force, and that the force required to make the body B of four pounds weight rise up one yard will make the body A of one pound weight rise up (not four yards, as Mr. Leibniz represents, but) sixteen yards, in quadruple the time. For the gravity of four pounds weight in one part of time acts as much as the gravity of one pound weight in four parts of time.

But Mr. Herman, in his *Phoronomia* [Amsterdam, 1716], p. 113 (arguing for Mr. Leibniz against those who hold that the forces acquired by falling bodies are proportional to the times of falling, or to the velocities acquired) represents that this is founded upon a false supposition: that bodies thrown upwards receive from the gravity which resists them an equal number of impulses in equal times. This is as much as to say that gravity is not uniform and, by consequence, to overthrow the theory of Galileo concerning projectiles, allowed by all geometers. I suppose that he means that the swifter the motion of bodies is upwards, the more numerous are the impulses, because the bodies meet the (imaginary) gravitating particles. And thus the weight of bodies will be greater when they move upwards and less when they move downwards. And yet Mr. Leibniz and Mr. Herman themselves allow that gravity in equal times generates equal velocities in descending bodies and takes away equal velocities in ascending bodies, and therefore is uniform. In its action upon bodies for generating velocity, they allow it to be uniform, in its action upon them for generating impulsive force, they deny it to be uniform, and so are inconsistent with themselves.

If the force acquired by a body in falling is as the space described, let the time be divided into equal parts, and if in the first part of time it gain one part of force, in the two first parts of time it will gain four parts of force, in the three first parts of time it will gain nine parts of force, and so on. And by consequence, in the second part of time it will gain three parts of force, in the third part of time it will gain five parts of force, in the fourth part of time it will gain seven parts of force, and so on. And therefore if the action of gravity for generating these forces is supposed, in the middle of the first part of time, to be of one degree, it will, in the middle of the second, third, and fourth parts of time, be of three, five, and seven degrees, and so on; that is, it will be proportional to the time and to the velocity acquired, and, by consequence, in the beginning of the time it will be none at all, and so the body, for lack of gravity, will not fall down. And by the same way of arguing, when a body is thrown upwards, its gravity will decrease as its velocity decreases and cease when the body ceases to ascend, and then for lack of gravity, it will rest in the air and fall down no more. So full of absurdities is the notion of this learned author in this particular.

To decide this question demonstratively, let two pendulous globes of hardened steel be suspended by equal radii or threads of equal length, so that when they

96 and 97. Here this learned author refers only to what he has said elsewhere, and I am also willing to do the same.

98. If the soul is a substance that fills the sensorium or place in which it perceives the images of things conveyed to it, still it does not follow from this that it must consist of corporeal parts (for the parts of body are distinct substances independent of each other), but the whole soul sees, and the whole hears and the whole thinks, as being essentially one individual.

99. In order to show that the *active forces* in the world[155] (meaning the quantity of motion[156] or impulsive force given to bodies) do not naturally diminish, this learned writer urges that two soft inelastic bodies meeting together with equal and contrary forces do for this only reason lose each of them the motion of their whole, because it is communicated and dispersed into a motion of their small parts. But the question is, when two perfectly **hard** inelastic bodies lose their whole motion by meeting together, what then becomes of the motion or active impulsive force? It cannot be dispersed among the parts, because the parts are capable of no tremulous motion for lack of elasticity. And if it is denied that the bodies would lose the motion of their wholes, I answer, then it would follow that elastic hard bodies would reflect with a double force, namely, the force arising from the elasticity, and moreover all (or at least part of) the original direct force—which is contrary to experience.

At length (upon the demonstration I cited from Sir Isaac Newton), he is obliged to (sec. 99) allow that the quantity of motion in the world is not always the same, and goes to another refuge, that motion and force are not always the same in quantity. But this is also contrary to experience. For the force here spoken of is not the *vis inertiae*[157] of matter (which

----

hang down and touch each other the radii or threads may be parallel. Let one of the globes be constantly the same and be drawn aside from the other to one and the same distance in all the subsequent trials. Let the other be of any size and be drawn aside the contrary way to a distance reciprocally proportional to its weight. Let both of them then be let go at one and the same moment of time, so that they may meet each other at the lowest place of their descent, where they hung before they were drawn aside; and the first globe will always rebound alike from the other. For this reason the force of the other is always the same when its velocity is reciprocally proportional to its weight. And by consequence, if its weight remains the same, its force will be proportional to its velocity. Q. E. D.

155. Clarke refers to the footnote in sec. 13 of his *Third Replies*.

156. Clarke refers to his footnote in sec. 93–5.

157. Clarke notes: The *vis inertiae* of matter is that passive force by which it always continues of itself in the state it is in and never changes that state but in proportion to a contrary power acting upon it. It is that passive force not by which (as Mr.

continues indeed always the same, as long as the quantity of matter continues the same), but the force meant here is relative active impulsive force, which is always proportional to the quantity of relative motion,[158] as is constantly evident in experience, except where some error has been committed in not rightly computing and subducting the contrary or impeding force, which arises from the resistance of fluids to bodies moved any way and from the continual contrary action of gravitation on bodies thrown upwards.

100–102. That active force,[159] in the sense defined above, does naturally diminish continually in the material universe has been shown in the last paragraph. That this is no defect is evident because it is only a consequence of matter being lifeless, void of motivity, inactive and inert. For the inertia of matter causes not only (as this learned author observes) that velocity decreases in proportion as quantity of matter increases (which is indeed no decrease of the quantity of motion), but also that solid and perfectly hard bodies, void of elasticity, meeting together with equal and contrary forces, lose their whole motion and active force (as has been shown above), and must depend on some other cause for new motion.

103. That none of the things here referred to are defects I have largely shown in my former papers. For why was not God at liberty to make a world that should continue in its present form as long or as short a time as he thought fit, and should then be altered (by such changes as may be very wise and fit and yet impossible perhaps to be performed by mechanism) into whatever other form he himself pleased? Whether my inference from

---

Leibniz understands it from Kepler) matter resists motion, but by which it equally resists any change from the state it is in, either of rest or motion, so that the very same force, which is required to give any certain velocity to any certain quantity of matter at rest, is always exactly required to reduce the same quantity of matter from the same degree of velocity to a state of rest again. This *vis inertiae* is always proportional to the quantity of matter, and therefore continues invariably the same in all possible states of matter, whether at rest or in motion, and is never transferred from one body to another. Without this *vis*, the least force would give any velocity to the greatest quantity of matter at rest, and the greatest quantity of matter in any velocity of motion would be stopped by the least force without any the least shock at all. So that properly and indeed all force in matter, either at rest or in motion, all its action and reaction, all impulse and all resistance, is nothing but this *vis inertiae* in different circumstances

158. Clarke notes: That is, proportional to the quantity of matter and the velocity, not (as Mr. Leibniz affirms, *Acta Eruditorum* 1695, p. 156) to the quantity of matter and the square of the velocity. See above, the footnote to sec. 93–5.

159. Clarke refers to the footnote above, sec. 93–5, and to his *Third Reply*.

this learned author's affirming[160] that the universe cannot diminish in perfection, that there is no possible reason which can limit the quantity of matter, that God's perfections oblige him to produce always as much matter as he can, and that a finite material universe is an impracticable fiction,[161] whether (I say) my inferring that (according to these notions) the world must necessarily have been both infinite and eternal is a just inference or not, I am willing to leave to the learned, who shall compare the papers, to judge.

104–106. We are now told that (sec. 104) space is not an order or situation but an order of situations. But still the objection remains that an order of situations is not quantity as space is. He refers therefore to sec. 54, where he thinks he has proved that order is a quantity, and I refer to what I have said above in this paper, in that section where I think I have proved that it is not a quantity. What he adduces concerning (sec. 105) time likewise amounts plainly to the following absurdity: that time is only the order of things successive and yet is truly a quantity, because it is not only the order of things successive but also the quantity of duration intervening between each of the particulars succeeding in that order. This is an express contradiction.

To say that (sec. 106) *immensity* does not signify boundless space, and that *eternity* does not signify duration or time without beginning and end, is (I think) affirming that words have no meaning. Instead of reasoning on this point, we are referred to what certain theologians and philosophers (that is, such as were of this learned author's opinion) have acknowledged, which is not the matter in question.

107–109. I affirmed that, with regard to God, no one possible thing is more miraculous than another, and that therefore a miracle does not consist in any difficulty in the nature of the thing to be done, but merely in the unusualness of God's doing it. The terms *nature,* and *powers of nature,* and *course of nature,* and the like, are nothing but empty words and signify merely that a thing usually or frequently comes to pass. The raising of a human body out of the dust of the earth we call a miracle, the generation of a human body in the ordinary way we call natural, for no other reason but because the power of God effects one usually, the other unusually. The sudden stopping of the sun (or earth) we call a miracle, the continual motion of the sun (or earth) we call natural, for the very same reason only of the one's being usual and the other unusual. If man did usually arise out of the grave as corn grows out of seed sown, we should certainly call that also natural, and if the sun (or earth) did constantly stand still, we

160. *Fourth Letter*, sec. 40, 20, 21, 22, and *Fifth Letter*, sec. 29.

161. See above, Leibniz's postscript to his *Fourth Letter*.

should then think that to be natural and its motion at any time would be miraculous. Against these evident reasons (*ces* (sec. 108) *grandes raisons*) this learned writer offers nothing at all, but continues barely to refer us to the vulgar forms of speaking of certain philosophers and theologians, which (as I before observed) is not the matter in question.

110–116. It is here very surprising that, in a point of reason and not of authority, we are still again (sec. 110) remitted to the opinions of certain philosophers and theologians. But to omit this, what does this learned writer mean by a (sec. 110) *real internal difference* between what is miraculous and not miraculous, or between (sec. 111) operations natural and not natural, absolutely and with regard to God? Does he think there are in God two different and really distinct principles or powers of acting and that one thing is more difficult to God than another? If not, then either a *natural* and a *supernatural action* of God are terms whose signification is only relative to us, we calling an usual effect of God's power *natural* and an unusual one *supernatural*, the (sec. 112) *force of nature* being, in truth, nothing but an empty word, or else by the one must be meant that which God does immediately himself, and by the other that which he does mediately by the instrumentality of second causes. The former of these distinctions is what this learned author is here professedly opposing, the latter is what he expressly disclaims (sec. 117), where he allows that angels may work true miracles. And yet besides these two, I think no other distinction can possibly be imagined.

It is very unreasonable to call (sec. 113) *attraction* a miracle and an unphilosophical term, after it has been so often distinctly declared[162] that by that term we do not mean to express the cause of bodies tending toward each other, but barely the effect or the phenomenon itself, and the laws or proportions of that tendency discovered by experience, whatever is or is not the cause of it. And it seems still more unreasonable not to

---

162. Clarke quotes the following passages in Newton, in which he denies that gravity is regarded as an occult quality:

"How these attractions may be performed, I do not here consider. What I call attraction may be performed by impulse or by some other means unknown to me. I use that word here to signify only, in general, any force by which bodies tend toward one another, whatever may be the cause. For we must learn from the phenomena of nature what bodies attract one another and what are the laws and properties of that attraction before we inquire into the cause by which the attraction is performed." *Optics,* beginning of Query 31.

"These principles I consider not as occult qualities . . . though the causes of these principles were not yet discovered." Query 31. See Appendix B, no. 3.

"Up to now we have explained the phenomena of the heavens . . . I frame no hypotheses." *Principia,* General Scholium. See Appendix B, no. 2.

admit gravitation or attraction in this sense, in which it is manifestly an actual phenomenon of nature, and yet at the same time to expect that there should be admitted so strange an hypothesis as the (sec. 109, 92, 87, 89, 90) *harmonia praestabilita,* which is that the soul and body of a man have no more influence on each other's motions and affections than two clocks,[163] which, at the greatest distance from each other, go alike without at all affecting each other. It is adduced indeed that God (sec. 92), foreseeing the inclinations of every man's soul, so contrived at first the great machine of the material universe as that, by the mere necessary laws of mechanism, suitable motions should be excited in human bodies as parts of that great machine. But is it possible that such kinds of motion,[164] and of such variety as those in human bodies are, should be performed by mere mechanism, without any influence of will and mind on them? Or is it credible that when a man has it in his power to resolve and know a month beforehand what he will do on such a particular day or hour to come, is it credible, I say, that his body shall by the mere power of mechanism, impressed originally on the material universe at its creation, punctually conform itself to the resolutions of the man's mind at the time appointed? According to this hypothesis, all arguments in philosophy taken from phenomena and experiments are at an end. For if the *harmonia praestabilita*[165] is true, a man does not indeed see, nor hear, nor feel anything, nor moves his body, but only dreams that he sees and hears and feels and moves his body.[166] And if the world can once be persuaded that a man's body is a mere machine, and that all his seemingly voluntary motions are performed by the mere necessary laws of corporeal mechanism, without any influence, or operation, or action at all of the soul on the body, they will soon conclude that this machine is the whole man, and that the soul in harmony in the hypothesis of a *harmonia praestabilita* is merely a fiction and a dream. Besides, what difficulty is there avoided by so strange a hypothesis? This only: that it cannot be conceived (it seems) how immaterial substance should act on matter. But is not God an immaterial substance? And does he not act on matter? And what greater difficulty is there in conceiving how an immaterial substance should act on matter than in conceiving how matter acts on matter? Is it not as easy to conceive how certain parts of matter may be obliged to follow the motions and affections of the soul without corporeal contact, as that certain portions of matter should be obliged to follow each other's motions by the

163. See Appendix A, no. 5.
164. See Appendix A, no. 13.
165. "Pre-established harmony."
166. See Appendix A, no. 12.

adhesion of parts, which no mechanism can account for, or that rays of light should reflect regularly from a surface which they never touch?[167] Of this, Sir Isaac Newton in his *Optics* has given us several evident and ocular experiments.

Nor is it less surprising to find this assertion again repeated in express words that, after the first creation of things (sec. 115–6), the continuation of the motions of the heavenly bodies, and the formation of plants and animals, and every motion of the bodies both of men and all other animals, is as mechanical as the motions of a clock. Whoever entertains this opinion is (I think) obliged in reason to be able to explain particularly by what laws of mechanism the planets and comets can continue to move in the orbs they do, through unresisting spaces, and by what mechanical laws both plants and animals are formed, and how the infinitely various spontaneous motions of animals and men are performed.[168] This, I am fully persuaded, is as impossible to make out as it would be to show how a house or city could be built, or the world itself have been at first formed by mere mechanism, without any intelligent and active cause. That things could not be at first produced by mechanism is expressly allowed, and, when this is once granted, why after that so great concern should be shown to exclude God's actual government of the world and to allow his providence to act no further than barely in concurring (as the phrase is) to let all things do only what they would do of themselves by mere mechanism, and why it should be thought that God is under any obligation or confinement either in nature or wisdom never to bring about anything in the universe, but what is possible for a corporeal machine to accomplish by mere mechanic laws after it is once set a going, I can no way conceive.

117. This learned author's allowing in this place that there is greater and less in true miracles, and that angels are capable of working some true miracles, is perfectly contradictory to that notion of the nature of a miracle,[169] which he has all along pleaded for in these papers.

118–123. That the sun attracts the earth through the intermediate void space, that is, that the earth and sun gravitate toward each other or tend (whatever is the cause of that tendency) toward each other with a force which is in a direct proportion to their masses, or magnitudes and densities together, and in an inverse duplicate proportion of their distances, and that the space between them is void, that is, has nothing in it which sensibly resists the motion of bodies passing transversely through, all this is noth-

167. See Sir Isaac Newton's *Optics*, Latin edition, p. 224, English edition, Book 2, p. 65.

168. See Appendix A, no. 13.

169. See above, Leibniz's *Third Letter*, sec. 17.

ing but a phenomenon or actual matter of fact found by experience. That this phenomenon is not produced (sec. 118) *sans moyen,* that is without some cause capable of producing such an effect, is undoubtedly true. Philosophers therefore may search after and discover that cause, if they can, whether it is it mechanical or not mechanical. But if they cannot discover the cause, is therefore the effect itself, the phenomenon, or the matter of fact discovered by experience (which is all that is meant[170] by the words attraction and gravitation) ever the less true? Or is a manifest quality to be called (sec. 122) *occult* because the immediate efficient cause of it (perhaps) is occult or not yet discovered? When a body (sec. 123) moves in a circle without flying off in the tangent, it is certain there is something that hinders it, but if in some cases it is not mechanically (sec. 123) explicable, or is not yet discovered what that something is, does it therefore follow that the phenomenon itself is false? This is very singular arguing indeed.

124–130. The phenomenon itself, the attraction, gravitation, or tendency of bodies toward each other (or whatever other name you please to call it by), and the laws or proportions of that tendency, are now sufficiently known by observations and experiments. If this or any other learned author can explain these phenomena by (sec. 124) the laws of mechanism, he will not only not be contradicted, but will moreover have the abundant thanks of the learned world. But, in the meantime, to (sec. 128) compare gravitation (which is a phenomenon or actual matter of fact) with Epicurus' declination of atoms (which, according to his corrupt and atheistic perversion of some more ancient and perhaps better philosophy was a hypothesis or fiction only, and an impossible one too in a world where no intelligence was supposed to be present) seems to be a very extraordinary method of reasoning.

As to the great principle of a (sec. 125, etc.) sufficient reason, all that this learned writer here adds concerning it is only by way of affirming and not proving his conclusion, and therefore needs no answer. I shall only observe that the phrase is of an equivocal signification and may either be so understood as to mean necessity only or so as to include likewise will and choice. That in general there (sec. 125) is a sufficient reason why everything is, which is, is undoubtedly true and agreed on all hands. But the question is whether in some cases, when it may be highly reasonable to act, yet different possible ways of acting may not possibly be equally reasonable, and whether, in such cases, the bare will of God[171] is not itself a sufficient reason for acting in this or the other particular manner, and whether in cases where there are the strongest possible reasons altogether

170. Clarke refers to the footnote in sec. 110–6.
171. See above, in sec. 1–20 and 21–5.

on one side, yet in all intelligent and free agents the principle of action (in which I think the essence of liberty consists) is not a distinct thing from the motive or reason which the agent has in his view. All these are constantly denied by this learned writer. And his (sec. 20 and 125, etc.) laying down his great principle of a sufficient reason in such a sense as to exclude all these, and expecting it should be granted him in that sense, without proof, this is what I call his *petitio principii,* or begging of the question, than which nothing can be more unphilosophical.

N.B. Mr. Leibniz was prevented by death from returning any answer to this last paper.

Appendices

A: Passages from Leibniz's Works That May Shed Light on Many Parts of the Previous Letters[1]

1. God, according to my opinion, is an extramundane Intelligence, as Martianus Capella[2] calls him, or rather a supramundane Intelligence.[3]

2. We must know that a spontaneity strictly speaking is common to us and all simple substances, and that, in an intelligent or free substance, this amounts to a dominion over its own actions. . . . By nature every simple substance has perception. . . .[4]

But active force contains a certain act or entelechy, and is something of a middle nature between the faculty of acting and act itself; it involves a *conatus* or endeavor, and is of itself carried into action and stands in need of no help, but only that the impediment is taken away. This may be illustrated by the examples of a heavy body stretching the string by which it is hung or of a bow bent. For though gravity or elasticity can and ought to be explained mechanically by the motion of ether, yet the ultimate cause of the motion in matter is a force impressed at the creation, which is in every part of matter but, according to the course of nature, is variously limited and restrained by bodies striking against each other. And this active faculty I affirm to be in all substance, and that some action is always arising from it, so that not even corporeal substance, any more than spiritual substance, ever ceases to act. This seems not to have been apprehended by those who have placed the essence of bodies in extension alone, or even in impenetrability, and who thought they could conceive of bodies as absolutely at rest. It will appear also from what I have advanced that one created substance does not receive from another the active force itself, but only the limits and determination of the endeavor or

---

1. Clarke's collection is selected from what Leibniz published in his lifetime, that is, from the *Theodicy* (1710; G VI and H) and from articles in the *Acta Eruditorum*, "On the Correction of Metaphysics and the Concept of Substance" (1694; G IV, 468–70 and L 432–4), "A Specimen of Dynamics" (1695; GM VI, 234–54 and AG 117–38), and "On Nature Itself" (1698; G IV, 504–16 and AG 155–67).

2. Martianus Capella, a Latin author of the late fifth century, known as the author of a kind of encyclopedia written in verse.

3. *Theodicy*, sec. 217, H 264.

4. *Theodicy*, sec. 291, H 304.

active faculty already preexisting in it.[5]

To act is the characteristic of substances.[6]

This primitive active power is of itself in all corporeal substance, for I think that a body absolutely at rest is inconsistent with the nature of things.[7]

On account of its form every body always acts.[8]

The active power, which is in the form, and the inertia, or resistance to motion, which is in the matter.[9]

Though I admit an active and, so to speak, vital principle superior to the common notion of matter everywhere in bodies.[10]

I have elsewhere explained, although it is a thing perhaps not yet well understood by all, that the very substance of things consists in the power of acting and being acted upon.[11]

So that, not only everything that acts is a single substance, but also every individual substance does perpetually act, not excepting even body itself, in which there is never any absolute rest.[12]

If we ascribe to our own minds an inherent force for producing immanent actions or, which is the same thing, for acting immanently, then it is no way unreasonable, in fact, to suppose that there is the same power in other souls or forms, or, if it is a better expression, in the natures of substances—unless a man will imagine that, in the whole extent of nature within the compass of our knowledge, our own minds are the only things with active powers, or that all power of acting immanently and vitally, if I may so speak, is joined to an intellect. These kinds of assertions, certainly, are neither founded on any reason nor can be maintained except in opposition to truth.[13]

Hence we may gather that there must be in corporeal substance an original entelechy or, as it were, a first subject of activity, that is, there must be in it a primitive motive power, which, being added over and above the extension (or that which is merely geometrical) and over and above the bulk (or that which is merely material), always acts, but yet is variously modified by the bodies striking against each other through conatus and

5. "On the Correction of Metaphysics and the Concept of Substance," L 433.

6. "A Specimen of Dynamics," AG 118.

7. "A Specimen of Dynamics," AG 119.

8. "A Specimen of Dynamics," AG 120.

9. "A Specimen of Dynamics," AG 124.

10. "A Specimen of Dynamics," AG 125.

11. "On Nature Itself," AG 159.

12. "On Nature Itself," AG 160.

13. "On Nature Itself," AG 161.

impetus. And it is that substantial principle, which in living substances is called soul and in other things the substantial form.[14]

Prime matter is indeed merely passive, but it is not a complete substance. To make it complete substance, there must be in addition a soul, or a form analogous to soul, or an original entelechy, that is, a certain urge or primitive force of acting, which is an inherent law, impressed by the decree of God. I think this opinion is not different from that of an eminent ingenious gentleman who recently maintained that body consists of matter and spirit, meaning by the word *spirit* not (as he does usually) an intelligent being, but a soul or form analogous to soul, and not a simple modification, but as something constituent, substantial, and enduring, what I usually call a monad, in which there is something like perception and appetite.[15]

On the contrary, I believe that it is consistent with neither the order nor beauty, nor reason of things that there should be a vital principle or power of acting immanently only in a very small part of matter, when it would be an argument of greater perfection for it to be in all matter. And nothing prevents there being souls or at least something analogous to souls everywhere, even if dominant and intelligent souls, such as are human souls, cannot be everywhere.[16]

What does not act, what lacks active force, what is void of discriminability, what lacks the whole ground and foundation for subsistence, can no way be a substance.[17]

3. Mr. Bayle has shown enough (in his *Reply to a Provincial,* chap. 139, pp. 748 *et seq.*) that the soul may be compared to a balance, where reasons and inclinations take the place of weights. According to him, the manner of our forming our resolutions may be explained by the hypothesis that the will of man is like a balance, which stands unmoved when the weights in both scales are equal and always turns on one side or the other in proportion as one scale has more weight in it than the other. A new reason makes a heavier weight, a new idea strikes the mind more vigorously than an old one. The fear of a great pain determines more strongly than the expectation of a pleasure. When two passions contend against each other, the stronger always remains master of the field, unless the other is assisted either by reason or some other contributing passion.[18]

14. "On Nature Itself," AG 162.
15. "On Nature Itself," AG 162–3.
16. "On Nature Itself," AG 163.
17. "On Nature Itself," AG 165–6.
18. *Theodicy,* sec. 324, H 321–2.

A man has always so much more difficulty in determining himself as the opposite reasons draw nearer to an equality, just as we see a balance turn so much the more readily as the weights in each scale are more different from one another. However, since there are often more than two ways to choose from, we may, therefore, instead of the balance, compare the soul to a force which has at one and the same time a tendency many ways, but acts on that part only where it finds the greatest ease or the least resistance. For example, air strongly compressed in a glass vessel will break it to get out. It presses upon every part, but finally makes its way where the glass is weakest. Thus the inclinations of the soul tend toward all apparent goods, and these are the antecedent acts of will, but the consequent will, which is the result, is determined toward that good which affects us the most strongly.[19]

4. There is never any such thing as an indifference *in equilibrium*, that is, where every circumstance is perfectly equal on both sides, so that there is no inclination to one side rather than the other.[20]

It is true, if the case [of the ass standing between two green fields and equally liking both of them] was possible, we would have to say that the ass would starve himself to death; but fundamentally the case is impossible, unless God brings about the thing on purpose.[21]

5. This is a consequence of my *system of a pre-established harmony*, which it may be necessary to give some account of here. The scholastic philosophers believed that the soul and body mutually affected each other by a natural influence, but since it has been well considered, that thought[22] and extended mass have no connection with each other, and are beings that differ *toto genere*, many modern philosophers have acknowledged that there is no *physical communication* between the soul and the body, despite the *metaphysical communication* always subsisting, by means of which the soul and the body make up one *suppositum*, or what we call a *person*. If there was any physical communication between them, then the soul could change the degree of speed and the line of direction of some motions in the body, and, vice versa, the body could cause a change in the series of thoughts that are in the soul. But such an effect as this cannot be deduced from the notion of anything we can conceive in the body and

19. *Theodicy*, sec. 324–5, H 322. See below, nos. 4 and 9.
20. *Theodicy*, sec. 46, H 148–9.
21. *Theodicy*, sec. 49, H 150. See above, no. 3, and below, no. 9.
22. Clarke notes that Leibniz "should have said the thinking substance for thought, or the act of thinking, is not a substance."

soul, though nothing is better known to us[23] than the soul, because it is most intimate to us, that is, most intimate to itself.[24]

I cannot help to arrive at the system which declares that God created the soul in such a manner at first that it must produce within itself and represent in itself successively what passes in the body, and that he has made the body also in such manner that it must of itself do what the soul orders. Consequently the laws that link the thoughts of the soul follow in the order of final causes and according to the evolution of perceptions arising within itself, must produce images that meet and harmonize with the impressions made by bodies upon our organs of sense; and the laws by which the motions of the body follow each other successively in the order of efficient causes likewise meet and harmonize with the thoughts of the soul, in such manner as that these laws of motion make the body act at the same time that the soul wills.[25]

Mr. Jaquelot has very well shown in his book on the *Conformity of Reason with Faith*, that it is just as if he who knows everything I shall order my footman to do tomorrow the whole day long should make a machine resemble my footman exactly and perform punctually everything I directed all day tomorrow; this would not at all hinder my freely ordering whatever I pleased, although the actions of my machine footman would not be in the least free.[26]

The true means by which God causes the soul to have sensations of what passes in the body arises from the nature of the soul, which represents bodies and is so constituted beforehand that the representations that are to arise in it, one following another according to the natural succession of thoughts, correspond to the changes that happens in bodies.[27]

6. In like manner, should it be the will of God that the organs of human bodies should conform to the will of the soul, according to *the system of occasional causes*, such a law would come into operation only through perpetual miracles.[28]

7. Indeed, we must admit, rather, that matter resists motion by a certain *natural inertia*, as Kepler properly named it, so that matter is not

23. Clarke notes: "As the eye does not see itself, and if a man had never seen another's eye, nor the image of his own in a glass, he could never have had any notion what an eye is, so the soul does not differ in its substance."

24. *Theodicy*, sec. 59, H 155.

25. *Theodicy*, sec. 62, H 157.

26. *Theodicy*, sec. 63, H 157.

27. *Theodicy*, sec. 355, H 339. See above, no. 2, and below, no. 11.

28. *Theodicy*, sec. 207, H 257. See below, no. 8.

indifferent to motion and rest, as is commonly supposed, but needs a greater active force to put it in motion, in proportion to its size.[29] There is natural *inertia* opposed to *motion*.[30] A certain sluggishness, so to speak, that is, an opposition to motion.[31] A sluggishness or resistance to motion in matter.[32] The experiments of bodies striking against each other, as well as reason, show that twice as much force is required to give the same speed to a body of the same kind of matter, but double in size.[33] This would not be necessary if matter was absolutely indifferent to rest and motion, and if that natural inertia I spoke of did not give it a sort of repugnance to motion.[34] It might be expected, considering the indifference of matter to motion and rest, that the largest body at rest could be carried away without any resistance by the smallest body in motion, in which case there would be action without reaction and an effect greater than its cause.[35]

8. That is why, if God made a general law that bodies should be attracted to one another, it could be put into operation only by perpetual miracles.[36]

9. The same may be said concerning perfect wisdom, which is no less orderly than mathematics, that if there was not a best (*optimum*) among all the possible worlds, God would not have made any at all.[37]

10. If we imagine two perfect and concentric spheres, perfectly similar both in the whole and in every part, the one enclosed in the other so as that there is not even the smallest gap between them, then, whether the enclosed sphere is supposed to revolve or is at rest, an angel himself (not to say more) could discover no difference between the state of these spheres at different times, nor find any way of discerning whether the

29. "On Nature Itself," AG 161.

30. "On Nature Itself," AG 161.

31. "A Specimen of Dynamics," AG 120.

32. "A Specimen of Dynamics," AG 124.

33. Clarke notes that "the author did not consider that twice as much force is also required to stop the same speed in a body of the same kind of matter, but double in size."

34. *Theodicy*, sec. 30, H 140–1.

35. *Theodicy*, sec. 347, H 333.

36. *Theodicy*, sec. 207, H 257. See above, no. 6.

37. *Theodicy*, sec. 8, H 128. See above, no. 4, and no. 3.

enclosed sphere is at rest, or revolves, or with what law of motion it turned.[38]

11. In my *system of pre-established harmony*, I show that by nature every simple[39] substance has perception, and that its individuality consists in the perpetual law that makes its appointed succession of perceptions arise naturally from one another, so as to represent to it its own body and, by the same means, the whole universe, according to the point of view proper to that simple substance, without its needing to receive any physical influence from the body. And the body likewise, on its part, acts correspondingly to the volitions of the soul by its own laws, and consequently only obeys the soul in correspondence with those laws.[40]

It must also be confessed that every soul represents to itself the universe according to its point of view and through a relation proper to it; but there is always a perfect harmony between them.[41]

The operation of spiritual machines, that is, of souls, is not mechanical, but it contains eminently whatever is excellent in mechanism; the motions that appear actually in bodies are concentrated by representation in the soul, as in an ideal world, which expresses the laws of the actual world and their consequences, but with this difference from the perfect ideal world which is in God, that most of the perceptions in human souls are but confused. For we must know that every simple substance embraces the universe in its confused perceptions or sensations, and that the succession of these perceptions is regulated by the particular nature of the substance, but in a manner which always expresses all universal nature. And every present perception leads to a new perception, just as every motion which such perception represents leads to another motion. But it is impossible for the soul to know distinctly its whole nature and consciously perceive how this innumerable number of little perceptions, heaped up, or rather concentrated together, are produced. To that end, it would be required that the soul understood perfectly the whole universe which is included within them, that is, it would have to be a God.[42]

12. The chain of causes connected one with another reaches very far. Hence, the reason alleged by Descartes to prove the independence of our

38. "On Nature Itself," AG 164.

39. Clarke had *single* for *simple* in the two occurences in this paragraph and the one in the second paragraph below.

40. *Theodicy*, sec. 291, H 304.

41. *Theodicy*, sec. 357, H 339.

42. *Theodicy*, sec. 403, H 365. See above, nos. 2 and 5.

free actions by what he calls an intense inward sensation is altogether inconclusive. We cannot, strictly speaking, be sensible of our independence, for we cannot always consciously perceive the often imperceptible causes on which our resolutions depend. It is as if a magnetic needle was sensible of and pleased with its turning toward the north; for it would believe that it turned itself, independently of any other cause, not consciously perceiving the insensible motions of the magnetic matter.[43]

13. An infinite number of great and small motions, internal and external, concur with us, which most often we do not consciously perceive. And I have already said that when someone walks out of a room, there are such reasons that determine him to set one foot forward rather than the other, without his reflecting on it.[44]

B: Selections from Newton's Works[45]

1. *Principia*, Scholium to Definitions

Up to now I have defined terms that are less known and explained the sense I would have them understood in the following discourse. I do not define time, space, place, and motion, since they are well known to all. Only I must observe that the common people conceive those quantities under no other notions than from their relation to sensible objects. And from this certain prejudices arise, for the removing of which it will be convenient to distinguish the terms into absolute and relative, true and apparent, mathematical and common.

I. Absolute, true, and mathematical time, of itself, and from its own nature, flows uniformly without relation to anything external, and by another name is called *duration*. Relative, apparent, and common time is some sensible and external (whether accurate or varying in rate) measure of duration by the means of motion, which is commonly used instead of true time, such as an hour, a day, a month, a year.

43. *Theodicy*, sec. 49–50, H 150–1. See below, no. 13.

44. *Theodicy*, sec. 46, H 149. See above, no. 12.

45. The selections from the *Principia* are from Motte's translation from the Latin in *The mathematical principles of natural philosophy* . . . (1729), modified. Passages added in the third edition (1726) are indicated by angle brackets in the text. The selection from the *Optics* is taken from *Opticks: or, A treatise of the reflexions, refractions, inflexions and colours of light* (2nd ed. with additions, 1718; 1st ed., 1704; Latin trans. by Samuel Clarke, 1706), modified. Passages added in the second edition are indicated by angle brackets in the text.

II. Absolute space, in its own nature, without relation to anything external, always remains similar and immovable. Relative space is some movable dimension or measure of the absolute spaces, which our senses determine by its position to bodies and is commonly taken for immovable space, such as the dimension of subterraneous, aerial, or celestial space, determined by its position with respect to earth. Absolute and relative space are the same in form and magnitude, but they do not always remain numerically the same. For if the earth, for instance, moves, a space of our air, which relatively and with respect to the earth always remains the same, will at one time be one part of the absolute space into which the air passes, at another time it will be another part of the same, and so, absolutely understood, it will be continually changed.

III. Place is a part of space that a body takes up, and is absolute or relative according to the space. I say, a part of space, not the situation nor the external surface of the body. For the places of equal solids are always equal, but their surfaces, by reason of their dissimilar figures, are often unequal. Positions properly have no quantity, nor are they so much the places themselves as the properties of places. The motion of the whole is the same as the sum of the motions of the parts, that is, the translation of the whole out of its place is the same thing as the sum of the translations of the parts out of their places; and therefore the place of the whole is the same as the sum of the places of the parts, and for that reason it is internal and in the whole body.

IV. Absolute motion is the translation of a body from one absolute place into another, and relative motion the translation from one relative place into another. Thus in a ship under sail, the relative place of a body is that part of the ship the body possesses, or that part of the cavity the body fills, and which therefore moves together with the ship; and relative rest is the continuance of the body in the same part of the ship or of its cavity. But real, absolute rest is the continuance of the body in the same part of that immovable space, in which the ship itself, its cavity, and all that it contains, is moved. For that reason, if the earth is really at rest, the body which relatively rests in the ship will really and absolutely move with the same velocity which the ship has on the earth. But if the earth also moves, the true and absolute motion of the body will arise, partly from the true motion of the earth in immovable space, partly from the relative motion of the ship on the earth; and if the body moves also relatively in the ship, its true motion will arise, partly from the true motion of the earth in immovable space, and partly from the relative motions as well of the ship on the earth as of the body in the ship; and from these relative motions will arise the relative motion of the body on the earth. As if that part of the earth, where the ship is, was truly moved toward the east with a velocity of 10,010 units, while the ship itself, with a fresh gale and full sails, is carried toward the west with a velocity expressed by ten of those units, while a sailor walks in the ship toward the east, with one unit of the said velocity, then the sailor will be moved truly in immovable space toward the east with a velocity of 10,001 units, and relatively on the earth toward the west with a velocity of nine of those units.

Absolute time is distinguished from relative in astronomy by the equation or correction of the apparent time. For the natural days are truly unequal, though they are commonly considered as equal and used for a measure of time; astronomers correct this inequality that they may measure the celestial motions by a more accurate time. It may be that there is no such thing as a uniform motion by which time may be accurately measured. All motions may be accelerated and retarded, but the flowing of absolute time is not liable to any change. The duration or perseverance of the existence of things remains the same, whether the motions are swift or slow or none at all; and therefore this duration ought to be distinguished from what are only sensible measures of it, and from which we deduce it by means of the astronomical equation. The necessity of this equation for determining the times of a phenomenon is established as well from the experiments of the pendulum clock as by eclipses of the satellites of Jupiter.

As the order of the parts of time is immutable, so also is the order of the parts of space. Suppose these parts to be moved out of their places, and they will be moved (if the expression may be allowed) out of themselves. For times and spaces are, as it were, the places as well of themselves as of all other things. All things are placed in time as to order of succession, and in space as to order of situation. It is from their essence or nature that they are places, and it is absurd that the primary places of things should be movable. These are therefore the absolute places, and translations out of those places are the only absolute motions.

But because the parts of space cannot be seen or distinguished from one another by our senses, we use sensible measures of them in their stead. For from the positions and distances of things from any body considered as immovable, we define all places, and then with respect to such places, we estimate all motions, considering bodies as transferred from some of those places into others. And so, instead of absolute places and motions, we use relative ones, and that without any inconvenience in common affairs; but in philosophical disquisitions, we ought to abstract from our senses and consider things themselves, distinct from what are only sensible measures of them. For it may be that there is no body really at rest to which the places and motions of others may be referred.

But we may distinguish rest and motion, absolute and relative, one from the other by their properties, causes, and effects. It is a property of rest that bodies really at rest do rest in respect to one another. And therefore as it is possible that in the remote regions of the fixed stars, or perhaps far beyond them, there may be some body absolutely at rest, but impossible to know, from the position of bodies to one another in our regions, whether any of these do keep the same position to that remote body, it follows that absolute rest cannot be determined from the position of bodies in our regions.

It is a property of motion that the parts, which retain given positions to their wholes, do partake of the motions of those wholes. For all the parts of revolving bodies endeavor to recede from the axis of motion, and the impetus of bodies moving forwards arises from the joint impetus of all the parts. Therefore, if surrounding bodies are moved, those that are relatively at rest within them will partake of their motion. Because of this, the true and absolute motion of a body cannot be determined by the translation of it from those which only seem to rest; for the external bodies should not only appear at rest, but be really at rest. For otherwise, all included bodies, besides their translation from near the surrounding ones, partake likewise of their true motions; and though that translation was not made, they would not be really at rest, but only seem to be so. For the surrounding bodies stand in the like relation to the surrounded as the exterior part of a whole does to the interior, or as the shell does to the kernel; but if the shell moves, the kernel will also move, as being part of the whole, without any removal from near the shell.

A property related to the preceding is that if a place is moved, whatever is placed in it moves along with it; and therefore a body which is moved from a place in motion partakes also of the motion of its place. Upon which account, all motions, from places in motion, are no other than parts of entire and absolute motions, and every entire motion is composed of the motion of the body out of its first place, and the motion of this place out of its place, and so on, until we come to some immovable place, as in the aforementioned example of the sailor. Because of this, entire and absolute motions can be no otherwise determined than by immovable places; and for that reason I did before refer those absolute motions to immovable places, but relative ones to movable places. Now no other places are immovable but those that, from infinity to infinity, do all retain the same given position one to another, and upon this account must ever remain unmoved, and do as a result constitute immovable space.

The causes by which true and relative motions are distinguished from one another are the forces impressed upon bodies to generate motion. True motion is neither generated nor altered, but by some force impressed upon the body moved; but relative motion may be generated or altered without any force impressed upon the body. For it is sufficient only to impress some force on other bodies with which the former is compared, that by their giving way, that relation in which the relative rest or motion of this other body did consist may be changed. Again, true motion always suffers some change from any force impressed upon the moving body; but relative motion does not necessarily undergo any change by such forces. For if the same forces are likewise impressed on those other bodies, with which the comparison is made, that the relative position may be preserved, then that condition will be preserved in which the relative motion consists. And therefore any relative motion may be changed when the true motion remains unaltered, and the relative may be preserved when the true suffers some change. Thus, true motion by no means consists in such relations.

The effects that distinguish absolute from relative motion are the forces of receding from the axis of circular motion. For there are no such forces in a purely relative circular motion, but in a true and absolute circular motion, they are greater or less, according to the quantity of the motion. If a vessel hung by a long cord is so often turned about that the cord is strongly twisted, then filled with water and held at rest together with the water, at once, by the sudden action of another force, it is whirled about the contrary way, and while the cord is untwisting itself, the vessel continues for some time in this motion, the surface of the water will at first be even, as before the vessel began to move; but after that the vessel, by gradually communicating its motion to the water, will make it begin to revolve sensibly and recede gradually from the middle, and ascend to the sides of the vessel, forming itself into a concave figure (as I have experienced); and the swifter the motion becomes, the higher will the water rise, until at last, performing its revolutions in the same times with the vessel, it becomes relatively at rest in it. This ascent of the water shows its endeavor to recede from the axis of its motion, and the true and absolute circular motion of the water, which is here directly contrary to the relative, becomes known and may be measured by this endeavor. At first, when the relative motion of the water in the vessel was greatest, it produced no endeavor to recede from the axis; the water showed no tendency to the circumference, nor any ascent toward the sides of the vessel, but remained of an even surface, and therefore its true circular motion had not yet begun. But afterwards, when the relative motion of the water had decreased, its ascent toward the sides of the vessel proved its endeavor to recede from the axis; and this endeavor showed the real circular motion of the water continually increasing, until it had acquired its greatest quantity when the water rested relatively in the vessel. And therefore this endeavor does not depend upon any translation of the water in respect of the ambient bodies, nor can true circular motion be defined by such translation. There is only one real circular motion of any one revolving body corresponding to only one power of endeavoring to recede from its axis of motion as its proper and adequate effect; but relative motions in one and the same body are innumerable, according to the various relations it bears to external bodies, and like other relations are altogether destitute of any real effect, except insofar as they may perhaps partake of that unique true motion. And therefore in the system of those who suppose that our heavens revolving below the sphere of the fixed stars carry the planets along with them, the several parts of those heavens and the planets, which are indeed relatively at rest in their heavens, do yet really move. For they change their position one to another (which never happens to bodies truly at rest), and being carried together with their heavens, partake of their motions, and as parts of revolving wholes, endeavor to recede from the axis of their motions. For that reason relative quantities are not the quantities themselves, whose names they bear, but those sensible measures of them (either accurate or inaccurate), which are commonly used instead of the measured quantities themselves. And if the meaning of words is to be determined by their use, then by the names time, space, place, and motion, their sensible measures are properly to be understood; and the expression will be unusual, and purely mathematical, if the measured quantities themselves are meant. On this account, those who interpret these words for the measured quantities violate the accuracy of language, which ought to be kept precise. Nor do those who confound real quantities with their relations and sensible measure defile the purity of mathematical and philosophical truths any less.

It is indeed a matter of great difficulty to discover and effectually to distinguish the true motions of particular bodies from the apparent, because the parts of that immovable space in which those motions are performed do by no means come under the observation of our senses. Yet the thing is not altogether desperate; for we have some arguments to guide us, partly from the apparent motions, which are the differences of the true motions, partly from the forces, which are the causes and effects of the true motions. For instance, if two globes, kept at a given distance one from the other by means of a cord that connects them, were revolved about their common center of gravity, we might, from the tension of the cord, discover the endeavor of the globes to recede from the axis of their motion, and from this we might compute the quantity of their circular motions. And then if any equal forces should be impressed at once on the alternate faces of the globes to augment or diminish their circular motions, from the increase or decrease of the tension of the cord, we might infer the increase or decrease of their motions; and hence would be found on what faces those forces ought to be impressed, that the motions of the globes might be most augmented, that is, we might discover their hindmost faces, or those which do follow in the circular motion. But the faces which follow being known, and consequently the opposite ones that precede, we should likewise know the determination of their motions. And thus we might find both the quantity and the determination of this circular motion, even in an immense vacuum, where there was nothing external or sensible with which the globes could be compared. But now, if some remote bodies that kept always a given position one to another were placed in that space, as the fixed stars do in our regions, we could not indeed determine, from the relative translation of the globes among those bodies, whether the motion did belong to the globes or to the bodies. But if we observed the cord and found that its tension was that very tension which the motions of the globes required, we might conclude the motion to be in the globes and the bodies to be at rest; and then, lastly, from the translation of the globes among the bodies, we should find the determination of their motions. But how we are to obtain the true motions from their causes, effects, and apparent differences, and the converse, shall be explained more at large in the following treatise. For to this end it was that I composed it.

2. *Principia*, General Scholium[46]

The hypothesis of vortices is pressed by many difficulties. In order that any planet may describe areas proportional to the time by a radius drawn to the sun, the periodic times of the parts of the vortices should observe the square of their distances from the sun; but in order that the periodic times of the planets may obtain the 3/2th power of their distances from the sun, the periodic times of the parts of the vortex ought to be as the 3/2th power of their distances. In order that the smaller vortices may maintain their lesser revolutions about Saturn, Jupiter, and other planets, and float quietly and undisturbed in the greater vortex of the sun, the periodic times of the parts of the solar vortex should be equal. But the rotation of the sun and planets about their axes, which ought to correspond with the motions of their vortices, are in disagreement with all these ratios. The motions of the comets are exceedingly regular, are governed by the same laws as the motions of the planets, and cannot be accounted for by the hypothesis of vortices. For comets are

46. The General Scholium was added in the 2nd ed., 1713.

carried in highly eccentric motions through all parts of the heavens, which is incompatible with the notion of a vortex.

Projectiles in our air feel only the resistance of the air. If the air is removed, as is done in Mr. Boyle's vacuum, the resistance ceases, for a bit of fine down and a piece of solid gold fall with equal velocity in this void. And the same argument must apply to the celestial spaces above the earth's atmosphere; in these spaces, where there is no air to resist their motions, all bodies will move with complete freedom and the planets and comets will constantly revolve in orbits given in shape and position, according to the laws above explained. But although these bodies may, indeed, carry on in their orbits by the mere laws of gravity, they could by no means have attained the regular position of the orbits through these laws.

The six primary planets revolve about the sun in circles concentric with the sun, in the same direction of motion and almost in the same plane. Ten moons revolve about the earth, Jupiter, and Saturn in concentric circles, in the same direction of motion, and nearly in the planes of the orbits of those planets. But it is not to be conceived that mere mechanical causes could give birth to so many regular motions, since the comets range over all parts of the heavens in very eccentric orbits. In this kind of motion, the comets pass easily through the orbits of the planets and with great rapidity; and at their aphelions, where they move the slowest and delay the longest, they recede to the greatest distances from each other, and hence suffer the least disturbance from their mutual attractions. This most beautiful system of the sun, planets, and comets could only proceed from the counsel and dominion of an intelligent and powerful Being. And if the fixed stars are the centers of similar other systems, since these are formed by the same counsel, they must all be subject to the dominion of One, especially since the light of the fixed stars is of the same nature as the light of the sun and light passes into all the other systems from every system <; and so that the systems of the fixed stars should not fall on each other by their gravity, he has placed those systems at immense distances from one another>.

This Being governs all things, not as the soul of the world, but as Lord over all; and because of his dominion he is usually called Lord God *Pantokrator*, or Universal Ruler. For God is a relative word, and is relative to servants, and Deity is the dominion of God, not over his own body, as those imagine who imagine God to be the world soul, but over servants. The supreme God is a Being eternal, infinite, absolutely perfect; but a being, however perfect, without dominion, cannot be said to be Lord God. For we say, my God, your God, the God of Israel, <the God of Gods, and Lord of Lords,> but we do not say, my Eternal, your Eternal, the Eternal of Israel <, the Eternal of Gods; we do not say, my Infinite or my Perfect>. These are titles which have no relation to servants. The word God[47] usually signifies Lord, but not every Lord is God. It is the dominion of a spiritual being that constitutes God—a true, supreme, or imaginary dominion makes a true, supreme, or imaginary God. From his true dominion it follows that the true God is a living, intelligent, and powerful Being, and, from his other perfections, that he is supreme or most perfect. He is eternal and infinite, omnipotent and omniscient; that is, he endures from eternity to eternity and is present from infinity to infinity; he governs all things and knows all things that are or can be done. He is not eternity and infinity, but eternal and infinite; he is not duration and space, but he endures and is present. He endures forever and is present everywhere, and, by existing always and everywhere, he constitutes duration and space. Since every particle of space is always, and every indivisible moment of duration is everywhere, certainly the Maker and Lord of all things cannot be never and nowhere. <Every sentient soul is still the same indivisible person at different times and in different organs of sense and motion. Successive parts are given in duration, coexistent parts in space, but neither is given in the person of a man or his thinking principle, and much less can they be found in the thinking substance of God. Every person, insofar as he is a sentient being, is one and the same person during his whole life, in each and all of his organs of sense. God is the same God always and everywhere.> God is omnipresent not only virtually, but also substantially, for virtues cannot subsist without substance. In him[48] are all things contained and moved, yet neither affects the other. God is not affected by the motion of bodies and bodies do not experience any resistance from God's omnipresence. It is allowed by all that the supreme God exists necessarily, and by the same necessity he exists always

47. Newton's marginal note: "Dr. Pocock derives the Latin word *Deus* from the Arabic *du* (in the oblique case *di*), which signifies the Lord. And in this sense princes are called gods, Psalm 84.6 and John 10.45. And Moses is called a god to his brother Aaron and a god to Pharaoh (Exodus 4.16 and 7.1). And in the same sense the souls of dead princes were formerly called gods by the heathens, but falsely, because of their lack of dominion."

48. Newton's marginal note: "This was the opinion of the ancients, such as Pythagoras (in Cicero, *On the Nature of the Gods,* book 1), Thales, Anaxagoras, Virgil (*Georgics* 4.220 and *Aeneid* 6.721), Philo (*Allegories,* at the beginning of book 1) Aratus (*Phenomena,* at the beginning). So also the sacred writers, as Saint Paul (*Acts* 17.27–28), Saint John 14.2, Moses (*Deuteronomy* 4.39 and 10.14), David (Psalm 139.7–9), Solomon (*1 Kings* 8.27), Job 22.12–14, Jeremiah 23.23–24. Moreover, the idolaters supposed that the sun, moon, and stars, the souls of men, and other parts of the world are parts of the Supreme God, and are therefore to be worshipped, but falsely."

and everywhere. Hence also he is all similar, all eye, all ear, all brain, all arm, all power to perceive, to understand, and to act, but in a manner not at all human, in a manner not at all corporeal, in a manner entirely unknown to us. As a blind man has no idea of colors, so have we no idea of the manner by which the all-wise God perceives and understands all things. He is entirely void of all body and bodily shape, and therefore cannot be seen, nor heard, nor touched; nor ought he be worshipped under the image of any corporeal thing. We have ideas of his attributes, but we do not know what the real substance of anything is. We see only the shapes and colors of bodies, we hear only sounds, we touch only the external surfaces, we smell only the odors, and taste the flavors; we do not know the inmost substances by our senses or by any act of reflection; much less, then, do we have any idea of the substance of God. We know him only through his most wise and excellent contrivances of things and final causes; we admire him for his perfections, but we revere and adore him on account of his dominion. <For we adore him as his servants, and a god without dominion, providence, and final causes is nothing else but fate and nature. No variation of things can arise from blind metaphysical necessity, which is certainly the same always and everywhere. All the diversity of natural things that we find suited to different times and places could only have arisen from the ideas and will of a Being existing necessarily. But, by way of allegory, God is said to see, to speak, to laugh, to love, to hate, to desire, to give, to receive, to rejoice, to be angry, to fight, to frame, to work, to build. For all our notions of God are taken from the ways of mankind by a certain similitude, which, though not perfect, has some likeness, however>. And this much concerning God, about whom a discourse from the appearances of things does certainly belong to natural philosophy.

Up to now we have explained the phenomena of the heavens and of our sea through the force of gravity, but have not yet assigned the cause for this. It is certain that it must proceed from a cause that penetrates to the very centers of the sun and planets with no diminution of force, and that operates, not according to the quantity of the surfaces of the particles upon which it acts (as mechanical causes usually do), but according to the quantity of the solid matter they contain, and which acts at immense distances, extended everywhere, always decreasing as the inverse square of the distances. Gravitation toward the sun is made up out of the gravitations toward the individual particles of the body, and in receding from the sun decreases precisely as the inverse square of the distances as far as the orbit of Saturn, as is evident from the aphelions of the planets being at rest, and even to the remotest aphelions of the comets, if those aphelions are also at rest. But up to now I have not been able to deduce the reason for these properties of gravity from phenomena, and I frame no hypotheses. For whatever is not deduced from the phenomena is to be called a hypothesis, and hypotheses, whether metaphysical or physical, whether of occult qualities or mechanical, have no place in experimental philosophy. In this philosophy, particular propositions are deduced from the phenomena and are rendered general by induction. The impenetrability, mobility, and impetus of bodies, and the laws of motion and of gravitation, were discovered in this way. And it is enough that gravity does really exist and acts according to the laws we have explained, and abundantly serves to account for all the motions of the celestial bodies and of our sea.

And now we might add something about a certain extremely subtle spirit that pervades and lies hidden in all gross bodies, by whose force and action the particles of bodies attract one another at near distances and cohere, if brought into contact, and electric bodies act at greater distances, both repelling and attracting neighboring corpuscles, and light is emitted, reflected, refracted, inflected, and heats bodies, and all sensation is aroused, and the members of animals move by the will, that is, by the vibrations of this spirit, propagated through the solid filaments of the nerves from the external organs of sense to the brain, and from the brain to the muscles. But these things cannot be explained in a few words, nor do we have at hand sufficient experiments by which the laws of action of this electric and elastic spirit can accurately be determined and demonstrated.

3. *Optics*, end of Query 31

And thus nature will be very conformable to herself and very simple, performing all the great motions of the heavenly bodies by the attraction of gravity that intercedes between those bodies, and almost all the small ones of their particles by some other attractive and repelling powers which intercede between the particles. The *vis inertiae* is a passive principle by which bodies persist in their motion or rest, receive motion in proportion to the force impressing it, and resist as much as they are resisted. By this principle alone there never could have been any motion in the world. Some other principle was necessary for putting bodies into motion; and now that they are in motion, some other principle is necessary for conserving the motion. For from the various composition of two motions, it is very certain that there is not always the same quantity of motion in the world. For if two globes joined by a slender rod revolve about their common center of gravity with a uniform motion, while that center moves on uniformly in a right line drawn in the plane of their circular motion, the sum of the motions of the two globes, as often as the globes are in the right line described by their common center of gravity,

will be bigger than the sum of their motions, when they are in a line per-
pendicular to that right line. By this instance it appears that motion may
be gotten or lost. But by reason of the tenacity of fluids and attrition of
their parts, and the weakness of elasticity in solids, motion is much more
apt to be lost than gotten, and is always upon the decay. For bodies which
are either absolutely hard or so soft as to be void of elasticity will not
rebound from one another. Impenetrability makes them only stop. If two
equal bodies meet directly *in vacuo*, they will by the laws of motion stop
where they meet and lose all their motion, and remain in rest unless they
are elastic and receive new motion from their spring. If they have so much
elasticity as suffices to make them rebound with a quarter, or half, or three
quarters of the force with which they come together, they will lose three
quarters or half or a quarter of their motion. And this may be tried by let-
ting two equal pendulums fall against one another from equal heights. If
the pendulums are of lead or soft clay, they will lose all or almost all their
motions; if they are of elastic bodies they will lose all but what they
recover from their elasticity. If it is said that they can lose no motion but
what they communicate to other bodies, the consequence is that *in vacuo*
they can lose no motion, but when they meet they must go on and penetrate one another's dimensions. If three equal round vessels are filled, the
one with water, the other with oil, the third with molten pitch, and the
liquors are stirred about alike to give them a vortical motion, the pitch by
its tenacity will lose its motion quickly, the oil being less tenacious will
keep it longer, and the water being less tenacious will keep it longest but
yet will lose it in a short time. From this it is easy to understand that if
many contiguous vortices of molten pitch were each of them as large as
those which some suppose to revolve about the sun and fixed stars, as
large as the Cartesian vortices, yet these and all their parts would, by their
tenacity and stiffness, communicate their motion to one another until
they all rested among themselves. Vortices of oil or water, or some more
fluid matter, might continue longer in motion, but unless the matter were
void of all tenacity and attrition of parts, and communication of motion
(which is not to be supposed), the motion would constantly decay. Seeing
therefore the variety of motion that we find in the world is always decreasing, there is a necessity of conserving and recruiting it by active principles, such as are the cause of gravity, by which planets and comets keep
their motions in their orbs and bodies acquire great motion in falling, and
the cause of fermentation, by which the heart and blood of animals are
kept in perpetual motion and heat, the inward parts of the earth are constantly warmed and in some places grow very hot, bodies burn and shine,
mountains take fire, the caverns of the earth are blown up, and the sun
continues violently hot and lucid and warms all things by his light. For we

meet with very little motion in the world besides what is owing either to these active principles or to the dictates of a will. <And if it were not for these principles, the bodies of the earth, planets, comets, sun, and all things in them, would grow cold and freeze and become inactive masses, and all putrefaction, generation, vegetation, and life would cease, and the planets and comets would not remain in their orbs.>

All these things being considered, it seems probable to me that God in the beginning formed matter in solid, massy, hard, impenetrable, moveable particles, of such sizes and figures, and with such other properties and in such proportion to space as most conduced to the end for which he formed them; and that these primitive particles being solids are incomparably harder than any porous bodies compounded of them, even so very hard as never to wear or break in pieces, no ordinary power being able to divide what God himself made one in the first creation. While the particles continue entire, they may compose bodies of one and the same nature and texture in all ages; but should they wear away or break in pieces, the nature of things depending on them would be changed. Water and earth, composed of old worn particles and fragments of particles, would not be of the same nature and texture now, with water and earth composed of entire particles in the beginning. And, therefore, that nature may be lasting, the changes of corporeal things are to be placed only in the various separations and new associations and motions of these permanent particles since compound bodies are apt to break, not in the midst of solid particles, but where those particles are laid together and only touch in a few points.

It seems to me further that these particles have not only a *vis inertia* accompanied with such passive laws of motion as naturally result from that force, but also that they are moved by certain active principles, such as is that of gravity and that which causes fermentation and the cohesion of bodies. These principles I consider, not as occult qualities supposed to result from the specific forms of things, but as general laws of nature, by which the things themselves are formed, their truth appearing to us by phenomena, though their causes are not yet discovered. <For these are manifest qualities and their causes are only occult. And the Aristotelians gave the name of occult qualities not to manifest qualities, but to such qualities only as they supposed to lie hidden in bodies and to be the unknown causes of manifest effects, such as would be the causes of gravity, and of magnetic and electric attractions, and of fermentations, if we should suppose that these forces or actions arose from qualities unknown to us and incapable of being discovered and made manifest. Such occult qualities put a stop to the improvement of natural philosophy, and therefore of late years have been rejected.> To tell us that every species of things is endowed with an occult specific quality by which it acts and produces manifest effects is to tell us nothing, but to derive two or three general principles of motion from phenomena, and afterwards to tell us how the properties and actions of all corporeal things follow from those manifest principles, would be a very great step in philosophy, though the causes of those principles were not yet discovered; and therefore I do not hesitate to propose the principles of motion above mentioned, since they are of very general extent <, and leave their causes to be found out>.

Now by the help of these principles all material things seem to have been composed of the hard and solid particles above mentioned, variously associated in the first creation by the counsel of an intelligent agent. For it became him who created them to set them in order. And if he did so, it is unphilosophical to seek for any other origin of the world, or to pretend that it might arise out of a chaos by the mere laws of nature, though being once formed it may continue by those laws for many ages. For while comets move in very eccentric orbs in all manner of positions, blind fate could never make all the planets move one and the same way in concentric orbs, some inconsiderable irregularities excepted which may have arisen from the mutual actions of comets and planets upon one another, and which will be apt to increase until this system needs a reformation. Such a wonderful uniformity in the planetary system must be allowed the effect of choice. And so must the uniformity in the bodies of animals, they having generally a right and a left side shaped similarly, and on either side of their bodies two legs behind and either two arms or two legs or two wings before upon their shoulders, and between their shoulders a neck running down into a backbone and a head upon it, and in the head two ears, two eyes, a nose, a mouth, and a tongue, similarly situated. Also the first contrivance of those very artificial parts of animals, the eyes, ears, brain, muscles, heart, lungs, midriff, glands, larynx, hands, wings, swimming bladders, natural spectacles, and other organs of sense and motion, and the instinct of brutes and insects can be the effect of nothing else than the wisdom and skill of a powerful ever-living agent, who, being in all places, is more able by his will to move the bodies within his boundless uniform sensorium, and thereby to form and reform the parts of the universe, than our spirit which is in us the image of God is able by our will to move the parts of our own bodies. <And yet we are not to consider the world as the body of God, or the several parts of it as the parts of God. He is a uniform being, void of organs, members, or parts, and they are his creatures subordinate to him, and subservient to his will; and he is no more the soul of them than the soul of man is the soul of the species of things carried through the organs of sense into the place of its sensation, where it perceives them by means of its immediate presence, without the intervention

of any third thing. The organs of sense are not for enabling the soul to perceive the species of things in its sensorium, but only for conveying them there; and God has no need of such organs, he being everywhere present to the things themselves.> And since space is divisible *in infinitum* and matter is not necessarily in all places, it may be also allowed that God is able to create particles of matter of several sizes and figures, and in several proportions to space, and perhaps of different densities and forces, and thereby to vary the laws of nature and make worlds of several sorts in several parts of the universe. At least, I see no contradiction in all this.

As in mathematics, so in natural philosophy, the investigation of difficult things by the method of analysis ought ever to precede the method of composition. This analysis consists in making experiments and observations, and in drawing general conclusions from them by induction, and admitting of no objections against the conclusions but such as are taken from experiments or other certain truths. For hypotheses are not to be regarded in experimental philosophy. And although the arguing from experiments and observations by induction is no demonstration of general conclusions, yet it is the best way of arguing which the nature of things admits of, and may be looked upon as so much the stronger by how much the induction is more general. And if no exception occurs from phenomena, the conclusion may be pronounced generally. But if at any time afterwards any exception shall occur from experiments, it may then begin to be pronounced with such exceptions as occur. By this way of analysis we may proceed from compounds to ingredients and from motions to the forces producing them, and in general from effects to their causes and from particular causes to more general ones, until the argument ends in the most general. This is the method of analysis; and the synthesis consists in assuming the causes discovered and established as principles, and by them explaining the phenomena proceeding from them and proving the explanations.

In the two first books of these *Optics* I proceeded by this analysis to discover and prove the original differences of the rays of light in respect of refrangibility, reflexibility, and color, and their alternate fits of easy reflection and easy transmission, and the properties of bodies, both opaque and pellucid, on which their reflections and colors depend. And these discoveries being proved may be assumed in the method of composition for explaining the phenomena arising from them; I gave an instance of this method in the end of the First Book. In this Third Book I have only begun the analysis of what remains to be discovered about light and its effects on the frame of nature, hinting several things about it and leaving the hints to be examined and improved by the further experiments and observations of such as are inquisitive. And if natural philosophy in all its parts, by pursuing this method, shall at length be perfected, the bounds of moral philosophy will be also enlarged. For so far as we can know by natural philosophy what is the first cause, what power he has over us, and what benefits we receive from him, so far our duty toward him as well as that toward one another will appear to us by the light of nature. And no doubt, if the worship of false gods had not blinded the heathen, their moral philosophy would have gone further than to the four cardinal virtues; and instead of teaching the transmigration of souls, and to worship the sun and moon and dead heroes, they would have taught us to worship our true author and benefactor, as their ancestors did under the government of Noah and his sons before they corrupted themselves.